'Can-do' is the attitude, meaning
and message of this book.

CHILDREN BEHAVE

A practical guide for parents

Virginia Hobart

Illustrations by Philippa Threlfall
Foreword by Ronnie Jackson Tanner

CHILDREN BEHAVE: A PRACTICAL GUIDE
Copyright © 2017 by Virginia Hobart
—First Edition—
ISBN-10: 0998065465
ISBN-13: 978-0998065465

The material in this book is intended for educational purposes. The author, publisher and distributors are not responsible in any manner for any harm or liability that may result from the use or misuse of the material presented herein.

This book was printed in the United States of America by Stirling Bridge Publications.

For Peter, with love

ACKNOWLEDGEMENTS

In chronological order, I must start with thanks to my parents for an extraordinary childhood in the country farm-school they built and ran in North Devon for more than thirty years. At Odam Hill, as well as classroom lessons, there was as much, or more, outdoor education, with nature study, animal care, tracking and other energetic games; the chance to climb trees, build camps and bonfires, or spend whole days exploring Exmoor and the coast

Then thanks to my Quaker high school in York (The Mount) for smoothing off a few rough edges before university's preparation for my work with London County Council Children's Department. This was wisely managed by Irene Sims from whom I was later to 'acquire' and learn much, from, Kate, my first foster child, as I also did after some years in Canada, while fostering teenage Jess.

Then, while supporting distressed families in North Devon I was, and still am, very grateful to my managers, Ronnie Jackson Tanner and Bernie Elkins for the chance and trust to work with troubled children in my own home. Several of them, discussed in the following pages, also deserve my thanks.

So do my friends: Colin Leys for urging me to write; Janet Ravenscroft and Kate Byrne for proof-reading/editing; and special thanks to my partner, Richard Howe for his constant belief and encouragement; to

Philippa Threlfall for her apt and lively illustrations; and finally to my son Peter, sometimes the subject, often the designer, and always the inspiration of this book.

CONTENTS

Acknowledgments

Foreword   1

PART ONE

Chapter One: Managing Children's Behaviour   6

Chapter Two: The Meaning of Behaviour   10

PART TWO

Chapter Three: Unacceptable Behaviour   16

Chapter Four: Looking Back   34

Chapter Five: Your Turn   40

Chapter Six: Right or Wrong?   42

PART THREE

Chapter Seven: Helping Children to Behave   50

Chapter Eight: All Purpose Suggestions and Ideas   70

Chapter Nine: Damage Control   72

Chapter Ten: Conclusion   80

MATTERS ARISING   82

   ADHD   150

   Bed Time   90

   Bed Wetting   146

   Biting   101

   Bullying   171

   Divorce and Separation   183

   Dummy or Thumb?   87

   Games   195

   Masturbation   97

   Mobile Phones   177

   Pets   190

   Picky Eaters   113

   Recipes   119

   Sex Education   138

   Siblings   157

Special Needs   163

Tantrums   106

When to Start Behaviour Management   83

Afterword   205

References and Resources   206

About the Author   215

FOREWORD

At home, within the family, a child should have a safe place in which to learn, experiment, make mistakes and have many successes. Providing such an environment for children is one of the most difficult and rewarding things a parent can do. Not everyone achieves it, and there is no such thing as perfection, but most of us manage 'good enough' parenting (Donald Winnicott). A minority of children, however, need keeping safe and some external help in learning to manage their own behaviour; and this is Ginny's area of expertise.

She and I first met at her cottage deep in the countryside. We sat outside in the sun and shared a lunch. Conversation was easy and comfortable: we talked about all kinds of things – her large and extended family, her experience of being a parent to her own and other people's children, working with children in the community who were not living with their own families; prior to that her work as a hospital social worker, living and working in Canada, and then returning to her English family and community to live and work.

This chat was an effort on my part to see whether we would have things in common, particularly in terms of underlying attitudes to children and their families, and where Ginny would fit within the community team. In the course of our conversation, it became apparent to me that she would be just perfect in the team, bringing specialist help to troubled children still living at home with their

VIRGINIA HOBART

families. This was a service we were being asked to provide but didn't have available in the area at the time.

Life is full of rules and these differ not only from culture to culture, but from home to home. And that is fine; consistency in the application of the rules is what really matters, and the certainty on our part as parents that the house rules are known and understood. More than one child has said, 'People are always telling me I'm doing it wrong, but no-one is telling me how to do it right'. This is when things can become so difficult for everyone – rules misunderstood, inconsistently applied, and too much or not enough responsibility given to the child. And in some instances there is conflict between the child and authority – at school or in the neighbourhood.

Working with these difficulties was Ginny's speciality, and she demonstrated consistency, reliability, kindness, fairness and sometimes absolutely breath-taking skill. As a member of our Family Support Team, she devised individual ways of working with children at odds with their family. These included, for each one, 'work' and play in *her* home which allowed them to discover and learn how to behave in *theirs*. Then, together, they would create a set of tools that would help them onto the path of self-management. Their satisfaction with these successes was often sufficient for them to choose to develop further the skills necessary for getting out of trouble. And eventually, with more active control over situations, to avoid trouble altogether.

Of course, the other important part of the work was to help the child's family to understand what was going on, and to spend time talking and showing how things could develop and improve for each family member. Ginny is always honest and direct, and loves to talk about her work. She also has a talent for writing. It is true to say that when her notes needed to be typed up there was never a shortage of volunteers, because everyone in the team was interested not only in how she worked, but also in 'what happened next'. The general interest and enthusiasm within the Children and Families teams for Ginny's work led to her being asked for input at evening classes for prospective adoption and foster parents.

But to limit the field is hardly fair on other parents who don't have access to those classes! This book is based on Ginny's materials, where she is very clear about the principles that inform her work, and the guidance she offers to support them. Of course, each group of 'students' had things they wanted to raise for themselves, many of which are included here, so the book is very much a genuine collaboration, and based on real life experiences.

There are many points made in this book which will resonate for you, the reader, and it is likely that different things will be highly relevant at different times for different readers. For me, at the moment, there are two really important things Ginny has said.

The first is not to ask for or expect gratitude from young children. "Years of care, attention, discipline and love are indeed *your* gifts, but are *their* birthright."

And the other: "No-one else knows, cares, thinks or worries as much about your children as you do, and it's the intention of this book to help you become experts in your own child care."

I think we are lucky to have access to these writings whose content can offer support with the most difficult and exciting job we shall ever have; I've loved reading it – I've written all over my copy, exclamation marks, comments and examples from my own parenting experiences. And then there are all the little sticky markers I've put on the pages I know I shall return to. Read the book, I can't recommend it highly enough.

—Ronnie Jackson Tanner
Family Services Manager
Devon County Council
January 2017

PART 1

CHAPTER ONE

MANAGING CHILDREN'S BEHAVIOUR

If, like me, you sometimes skip a book's introductory pages, you may find this one will make more sense once you know it is based on a behaviour management class I gave, for several years, to prospective adoption and foster parents (from here on, for the sake of brevity, these will be referred to as 'my students': probably not how they thought of themselves, so apologies to any who may be reading this).

There are many different ways to approach such a huge, and hugely important, subject: my preference was, and still is, to introduce the class – and now you – to a favourite role model of mine: a blond and beautiful mother of ten who knows all about managing the behaviour of her children. No wakeful nights for **her**, no picky eaters, no absconders, no vandalism, no back-chat, no public embarrassment or private angst.

Wonder woman or figment of her own imagination? Someone to admire and envy, or to scorn and dismiss as a deluded fraud? Well, you'll waste no time deciding when I point out that the most obvious difference between this and your ideal mother is her all-over body hair and extra pair of legs.

Even so, everything I have said about our collie dog Penny, who has no more training and experience than her own good mothering, is perfectly true. Probably she has learned more from several previous litters, but right from the first one she seemed to know what she needed to do. Offspring no sooner born than washed, fed and put down to sleep. From then on, no question who was in charge of nutrition, hygiene, toilet-training, squabble-solving in the kennel, before the gradual introduction of her friendly, well-mannered pups to the challenges and freedoms of the outside world.

Isn't that what we, as parents, would like to achieve for our own children? And why is it so much harder for us?

It is safe to say that much of Penny's success is down to instinct, her own good 'childhood' experience and, of course, to the less complicated needs and challenges of a dog's life.

So what about our instincts then? And the good example of our parents? Why isn't that enough even with our more complicated lives?

Actually in the days before widespread education, libraries, social workers and agony aunts, for many of our ancestors their instincts and their parents' example and support must have been enough, or not so many us would be here right now.

One thing lacking though, for today's double-income and increasingly mobile families, is the child-minding and guidance of grandparents, themselves often now working, traveling or otherwise out of reach. Taking the place of their traditional back-up is an ever growing host of 'experts' telling us what to think and do.

In as much as that label applies to me, I can assure you no one else knows, cares, thinks or worries about their children as much as you do, and it is the intention of this book to help you become experts in your own child care.

Experts, after only one class? Surely not.

Of course there's not one person, not one book, and not one evening class that can possibly cover all aspects and details of behaviour management. But yes, really, because it is a subject that can be simplified by breaking it down into three connecting parts (with a 'matters arising' section for occasional use at the end):

1. THE MEANING OF BEHAVIOUR

2. UNACCEPTABLE BEHAVIOUR

3. HELPING CHILDREN TO BEHAVE

Please don't find in the word 'simplified' any suggestion that child-rearing is going to be easy. We all know it is not, but it can be made less difficult with the knowledge of some basic principles and practice which are easy to grasp and helpful for parents to keep in their mental tool kit.

Something else we all know is that even high-quality tools aren't much use without at least a basic knowledge of the material intended for their work, and the same applies to even the best advice about managing behaviour without some understanding of the word itself.

CHAPTER TWO

THE MEANING OF BEHAVIOUR

When we hear the words 'behaviour' and 'children' in the same sentence most of us expect they will be followed by examples of the speaker's own, or other children's misdeeds.

Well, the Oxford English Dictionary defines behaviour as **'manners, observable actions and treatment shown to others'.** Notice nothing there about good or bad, nor any particular reference to children. This is because behaving is what, for better or worse, we all do throughout our lives.

Psychologists tell us all behaviour has a purpose. In most cases, this is to get something we want. If that sounds unacceptably selfish, just take a look at your own, dictionary-defined, behaviour. Ask yourself about the occasions when you are friendly, courteous, kind, fair, bossy, angry etc. and consider, in each case the possible pay-off of attention, affection, admiration, respect, or even simply just peace and quiet.

The same purpose can be claimed for even the most unsung and unselfish deeds being rewarded by feeling good in and about ourselves.

Adults, taking an honest look at their own actions, can usually give reasons and recognise the pay-offs for things they have and have not done. Children, however, especially when young, troubled or confused, often can **not**, and it is up to parents to interpret their behaviour before deciding how to react.

Most of us get the clues of other people's <u>body</u> language, but the '<u>behaviour</u> language' of children is not so widely recognised and understood.

I know that most parents are more concerned about the causes and cures of bad behaviour, and I'll come to that after first a brief look at the good.

The unspoken message of young children's good behaviour is usually some version of 'I'm OK, you're OK' [*] or 'I'm happy with what I – and you - are doing right now.'

At such times, how often are we relieved to see, and take, the chance to phone a friend, have a bath or start cooking the supper? Unfortunately, 'very often' is the likely answer from most parents, including me; all missing the opportunity to recognise and encourage this kind of 'goodness' with praise, a small treat or at least a smile and affectionate passing pat.

[*] The title of Dr. Thomas A. Harris's popular self-help book.

Meanwhile, and naturally, what usually gets attention is children's bad behaviour; in all its variations, challenging their parents' patience and understanding.

You will see I have no problem with the description of unruly behaviour as 'bad', but since today's parents are often advised to use the term 'unacceptable', from now on, if I remember, so be it. As, however, neither word should be used to describe any actual child, I shall digress a moment to tell you why.

Unacceptable behaviour and parents' response to it is an inevitable part of a child's learning experience. Probably all children, while young, will have told lies to get out of trouble, will have cheated to win a game, trashed toys in anger, stolen items from others or even from shops.

Of course parents are justified in punishing such behaviour, but NOT in naming the child as a klutz, liar, cheat, vandal, thief or all-round bad egg.

Once the 'crime' is forgiven and punishment's lesson learned, any such label is soon forgotten by the parents, but may be long-remembered by the child whose self-confidence and good intentions are undermined.

A much better remedy is the clearly made point that lying, cheating, stealing etc. will be punished and then forgiven for the chance of a clean sheet and a fresh start. Any reference to the child being, in these and other ways, bad, is unhelpful, unwise and all too likely to be self-fulfilling.

In short, the lesson for parents is **to label the action and not the child.**

Some psychologists advise the same sort of response to children's good behaviour since no child is able to be good all the time. Such well-meant labels as helpful, honest, clever, brave and kind may seem to set a standard that is impossible to maintain. Applied instead to the action, they will still give the encouragement of praise without adding, to the child's inevitable lapses, the extra guilt for the parents' disproved claim. I think there is something to be said for this advice, but not enough for me to include it in that bold type above.

P.S. One advantage of 'unacceptable' over 'bad' as a label is its evidence of forethought and specific discussion which once - maybe more than once - clearly explained, justifies the parents' firm response, and their children's, albeit grudging, respect.

After that digression we're done with Part 1 and ready for a closer look at different kinds of troublesome behaviour. Now here comes the longest, most challenging and significant part of this book, with a lot to take in that will probably require the occasional rest stop or coffee break.

PART 2

CHAPTER THREE

UNACCEPTABLE BEHAVIOUR

Those of you with children already have experience of this, while most parents-in-waiting will have some particular worries and concerns.

In my classes the students were invited to name the kind of 'playing-up' which they found, or expected to find, most difficult to 'manage'. This was to be their first step towards recognising common causes and effects, and then understanding the meanings and messages of their children's troublesome behaviour.

On the next page you'll see a typical contribution copied from a flip chart that soon had hands up all around the room after a couple of suggestions of mine to prompt and encourage the rest.

If this looks like a parent's worst nightmare, please remember it represents the combined dread of twenty-plus class members, and is by no means applicable to any one child. If you would like to make your own list (on the following page), here is something positive to keep in mind. When your children are not doing any of the things you have written down, it stands to reason they are being 'good'.

CLASS EXAMPLES OF UNACCEPTABLE BEHAVIOUR

disobedience

tantrums

bad language

bullying

biting   Picky eaters

refusing school

cruelty to animals

wont stay in bed

Stealing

not sharing

hitting and kicking

trashing own or others property

lying   bed-wetting

Kicking off in the supermarket

Scribbling on walls

running away

**YOUR EXAMPLES OF
UNACCEPTABLE BEHAVIOUR**

_____

_____

_____

_____

_____

_____

_____

_____

_____

_____

_____

_____

_____

_____

_____

_____

_____

_____

_____

_____

Before your next step along this road just take a moment to remember the description of children's behaviour as a form of self-expression with a language of its own. Meanwhile my next step is to remind you that hunger, fatigue, unrecognised aches, pains, griefs and disappointments can skew anyone's, even adults', best intentions, and provide at least a reason for misbehaviour, if not an actual excuse.

Another reason could be an undetected health problem, like that of a friend's six year-old daughter, frequently accused of ignoring parents' and teachers' instructions. Eventually she was taken to a doctor and found to have a rare form of epilepsy. This was causing brief 'absences' of which neither child nor parents were aware, and to which prescribed medicine put a speedy and happy end.

Aside from any such short or long-term cause and effect, here, from my experience, is a list of the seven most common meanings and messages of children's misbehaviour.

1. Give me more attention.

2. Give me more control over my life.

3. I am bored, give me something to do.

4. Can I get away with this?
   (Testing boundaries.)

5. I am confused/angry/frightened
   (Needing your help/control.)

6. Just copying my friends.*

7. Why not if you do?

* For parents adopting or fostering 'disadvantaged' children, number 6 was 'I don't know any better', but for you, 'just copying my friends' is likely to crop up often enough to be included here.

My class was asked to consider the list and then suggest which of the seven numbers fitted the examples written on the chart. This is something you might like to do on your own list, preferably before looking at the chart below which shows my students' response to theirs.

CLASS EXAMPLES OF UNACCEPTABLE BEHAVIOUR

Too many different answers? How's anyone supposed to make sense of all that?

Before you dismiss this result as a fat lot of use, just remember that these are the opinions and guesses of many people based on their experience of many children unknown to you. And don't forget that you do know – or will get to know very well - the child whose behaviour is your concern: the one who has been cooped up all day indoors, or been bullied at school; the one who is jealous of a new baby, who has been sick or having nightmares; who is lonely, bored, hungry or simply tired.

So please don't underestimate your own ability, based on your knowledge, to understand, or at least make a pretty good guess at, the meaning and messages of your child's behaviour.

> Debate about some of the flip chart examples could have gone on all evening and, without enough class time, there would often be a student or two staying late with particular interests or concerns. The most common of these will be discussed at length as Matters Arising at the end of the book.

Meanwhile this is the time for more comment about the most common 'messages' of children's unacceptable behaviour. Some of them are easy to understand, while others may need a bit of unpacking with perhaps the addition of some examples or advice. For instance:--

Number 3
I'm bored; give me something to do. No need for expensive trips or treats; any game or activity with family and friends will do very well, especially if it can be something energetic and tiring outside in the fresh air. The pay-off for parents could well be more good will during the day and less foot-dragging at bed time.

Number 4

Can I get away with this? It isn't only troubled or troublesome children who will test boundaries from time to time as, looking back, you can probably remember yourself. Hopefully, parents' authority is established and respected well before a child's wish or need to test it but, as time goes by or circumstances change, testing of new boundaries and limits is a normal and, depending on the parents' response, also useful learning experience for the child.

Number 5

I'm confused, angry or frightened and need your help and control. Your successful response to children in this state is going to depend on their age. For the very young, a gentle but firm hold on all flailing limbs may be enough, or else time out in some quiet place until both child and parent are ready to talk.

For older children a side-by-side conversation may be easier than face-to-face and eye-to (shifty or defiant)-eye. An example for many of us will be the most revealing and relieving confessions made, and forgiven, on the front seat of a moving car. Another is washing and drying dishes together after a meal, though less likely nowadays with machines for this job in most homes. Still there is a good chance of either of these measures ending with a cuddle or hand-shake and truce.

Number 6

Just copying siblings and friends. As this comes up in one of the following exercises, there is no need for more to be said here.

Number 7

Why not, if you do? Most parents find themselves sometimes saying or doing things in front of their children which it would be better if they had not. Things like swearing, smacking, smoking, being inconsistent or unfair. I know I have, and expect so also will you.

At such times the old-fashioned 'Do as I say, not as I do' really won't wash: an honest own-up and apology will certainly be better given and received.

> Much more, though, was needed from the parents once referred by Social Services for my help with their children's constant fighting, swearing, tormenting the dog and refusing to go to school. A few minutes into my first visit what I saw and heard was a stream of the parents' foul language, the dog getting kicked, the children getting punched and sworn at by the mother (not yet dressed) and father (clutching a bottle of beer) at 11 o'clock in the morning.
>
> Of course you don't need such an extreme example to get its all too obvious point that **our children's behaviour, whether or not 'acceptable', is usually a reflection of our own.**

By now you might be wondering why no reference has been made yet to numbers 1 and 2. The reason is that, in my experience, they are the most common causes of misbehaviour which I have left till last to be more easily remembered until – and long after - you have finished this book.

Quite a lot follows now that is important to be said, read and understood, so this might be a good time to for you to have a break: take a walk, a bath, a nap, or at least a nice cup of tea.

Number 1

Give me more attention: It may surprise you to hear that the attention of parents and carers is as important to the wholesome development of young children as food which, of course, everyone knows is necessary for good health, and if altogether withheld, for life itself.

But not everyone knows the evidence of many studies and some outrageous experiments, that even well-fed children who are denied a carer's individual, intimate and responsive attention are likely to miss their mental and social milestones, physically fail to thrive and, in extreme cases, even to die.

Perhaps some of you will have seen the TV coverage of a Romanian orphanage where typical mental and social symptoms like rocking, head-banging and empty-eyed hopelessness were defeating the best efforts of far too few staff.

Fortunately such institutional neglect is very rare in our world, but this example will help you understand that all children's need for attention is so vital to their well-being, they will go to any lengths to get it, if not by good behaviour, then by bad.

Please don't think this means that you have to dance attendance on your children all around the clock. Even if this were possible, it would not be good for either parent or child who certainly both benefit from some down-time by themselves.

Between organised activities, trips and treats, your passing smile, your interested question, thoughtful answer, compliment or kind touch will be enough for most children to occupy and amuse themselves with siblings, friends or even on their own.

Number 2

Give me more control over my life: The appropriate response to this appeal gives children the chance to make decisions for themselves, to learn from their mistakes, to gain from experience the confidence and self-respect that offer no challenge to the parents' own authority.

By 'appropriate response', I mean age- or stage-related, and recall the example of our Penny in full charge of 'gradually introducing her offspring to the challenges and freedoms of the outside world.' Like hers, the proper goal of human parents is to raise children who can be in charge and control of themselves.

I have emphasised the word gradually because, of course, maturity, the so-called age of discretion, doesn't just magically happen overnight. It is, however, a milestone that can be reached by parents taking - even making - opportunities all along the way for their children to practise and learn.

One of the controls that is easiest for parents to give, and most satisfying for children to take, is permission to make certain choices for themselves. Of course these should not include any that could be harmful to them or to any nearby person or thing.

Such choices need not be inconvenient to others, and had better not include too many options: to avoid lengthy dithering, 'either this or that' is usually enough.

Right from the start you will discover that even babies have preferences: such as how they are held, fed and put down to sleep which, keeping health and safety in mind, it is in the best interest of everyone present to allow.

The preferences of toddlers will be made loud and clear when it comes to things like story books at bed time, toys in the bath, swings and roundabouts in the playground and, all too often when you're hurrying to go out, what they want, and want not to wear. Let this last example stand for the rest: red socks or blue socks? <u>The choice matters more to the child</u> than to even the most fashion-conscious parent who, allowing it, may be rewarded by an easier time with all the other clothes.

Any one concerned about such 'permissiveness' raising a generation of little tyrants would be reassured by Roger Graef's 1997 documentary film 'Breaking the Cycle'. The setting was Swindon's Marlborough Day Centre where badly behaved children were being 'rehabilitated' so they could return to the nursery schools and play groups from which they had been expelled.

Along with parent counselling and other strategies, the staff were constantly taking **and** making opportunities to offer choices, with usually just two options: this or that toy, dress-up costume, craft kit, colour or flavour of the snack-time drink. Any hesitation to join others' misbehaviour, or any calm between personal storms, were recognised as the individual's choice and were rewarded with praise and a token in the child's special cup - all to be counted and admired at the end of the day.

This course of just ten weeks had a very high success rate with never a doubt from parents, student observers or the children themselves about who was in full charge and control.

I have often thought of the stage, sometimes known as 'the terrible twos', as a sort of mini-adolescence with, in each case, the child flexing healthy emotional muscles against no-longer wanted protection and control

The years between these naturally occurring rebellious stages are often the most easy and least stressful for parents. School-age children are absorbing knowledge like the proverbial sponge, and returning with no worse grievance than their loyalty to Miss or Sir's different take on this or that home truth.

At this stage evenings and weekends are all yours, when children will still benefit from the choices and freedoms you are prepared to grant: for instance homework before or after tea, gold fish or guinea pig, bath or shower, extra time or distance on the bike. The pay-off for parents here is less argument and more peace, while the challenge of decision, the consequence of a better or worse choice and the evident trust of adults all contribute to the child's confidence and self-respect.

As for adolescent behaviour, I have always been more concerned about the absence than the presence of that "flexing of healthy emotional muscles". Trying as it usually is, you can take heart from this observation:

"Young people today think of nothing but themselves. They have no respect for their parents and are impatient with all restraint. Boys talk as if they know everything, and what passes for wisdom with us is foolishness to them. As for girls, they are forward, immodest and unwomanly of speech, behaviour and dress."

—variously attributed to Socrates, Plato and Aristotle: apparently normal teenage behaviour in 3rd century BC Greece, one of the most successful and civilised societies of its time.

Overleaf you will find a visual representation of all that has been said so far about children's need for gradually increased control over their time and space: often hard for parents to judge, but SO important for every aspect of your child's development.

In the centre of each circle is your child at a particular age and stage. The surrounding white space indicates the freedoms and choices s/he may take for granted. Beyond that, the grey band with question marks is for whatever mental, physical and social growth justifies enlarging the existing space of white.

This should not be given, or taken, without discussion and negotiation which is, of course, another learned skill that increases confidence and self-respect. Then the thick black line is the limit not to be crossed until you, the parents, decide.

When ready, the child moves up a stage with a new grey band around the extended white space, in a process to be repeated throughout childhood and adolescence until the day when you find yourselves negotiating about things like alcohol, curfews and cars.

The good news to take on board before the next exercise is that children can be successfully raised under a number of different family regimes that suit the parents' standards and values, principles and personality. Whether strictly routine, flexibly relaxed or some middling compromise, none is intrinsically better or worse as long as parents have a good grasp of the only three things that really matter when it comes to the behaviour management of any family.

1. Decisions agreed and shared for their mutual support and united front.

2. Rules and standards that are consistently maintained so the children know what to expect.

3. Whatever their particular regime, it is the parents, not the children, who are in charge.

There is plenty of evidence of good, and not so good, child care being passed on from one generation to the next. The influence of our own childhood experience may be stronger than anything later learned from classes and books, on the kind of parents we ourselves are going to be.

I came across a striking example of this in my first job at a hospital outpatient department where a small boy was climbing over chairs and benches in the waiting room. It was the sound of angry adult voices that brought me from my nearby office in time to find the senior nurse berating the father for beating his son in the lavatory with his leather belt. Their parting shots went something like this: -

Father: Why not? It worked for my old man and never did me any harm.

Nurse: That cuts no ice with me, and it's not going to 'work' for you in my clinic ever again.

Young and inexperienced at the time, all I felt was admiration for the nurse and much relief for not being first on the scene. Several times since, when faced with that justification of corporal punishment, my response has been some version of the following: -

I don't know you well enough to comment on your claim of no harm, but I do know that family abuse of vulnerable old people is not uncommon, and that the day will surely come when your child is bigger and stronger, and you may well find yourself getting a taste of your own medicine.

Now then, back to the present. If, like our Penny's, your childhood experience was good, you are already prepared for the road ahead with your parents' example to follow and your own natural instincts to trust.

If you were not so lucky, you still have an ace up your sleeve: something not within reach of even the most intelligent of dogs. That is the ability to reflect on your childhood, to recognise and decide what to select and what to reject in terms of your parents' standards, values, strategies and rules.

The next exercise is for you to do just that. First a word, though, to any of the lucky ones who may think this unnecessary for them, and therefore something to skip.

Just remember the example, attitudes and methods of your parents were those of a previous generation. Since then enough time has passed for new ideas, different and more effective practices to influence good parents' choices and decisions. Now add to that the different childhood experience of your partner, and I hope you will decide to carry on from here.

Time for another break?

CHAPTER FOUR

LOOKING BACK

Successful management of your children's behaviour begins with the consideration of what you and your partner do and do not find acceptable. A good place to start on this is a thoughtful look at your own childhood experience.

This allows you to identify the positives and, since no one's childhood is perfect, also the negatives, of the way you were raised. Things like the amount of permitted freedom and self-control, expressions of affection, chores, pocket money, punishment, family traditions and rules all give clues to your parents' values and standards which may have been clearly spelled out or, with the canny perception of most children, have been simply understood.

With the passage of time, it is not so easy to recognise the **unspoken** values, attitudes and rules that are common to all families, expressed and reinforced with deeds rather than words. Here are some examples from my personal and professional experience which may prompt your own memories:-

• Might is right.

• The last word wins.

• Life's cup is always half empty, never half full.

• All problems are somebody else's fault.

• For social success it is more important to be amusing than accurate.

• Men and boys are more important than women and girls.

• Don't trust neighbours, foreigners or 'them'. (Meaning anyone in authority who is different and worse than us).

• Anything but the proper name for genitals. ('You know, down there').

Such messages, constantly given and received, are the more powerful for being unspoken, and therefore not up for challenge and choice.

Of course there are as many <u>positive </u>examples that family members show but don't tell: things like optimism, tolerance, trust without prejudice, community involvement, a wide welcome to friends and neighbours and, best of all, between parents and children the fairness, affection and respect that says more clearly than any words: 'I'm OK and you are OK too.'

It is important – arguably <u>more</u> important - for such hidden messages to be recognised and included in your choice of examples to be or not to be followed.

In my classes the chance to practice this kind of review was the purpose of the next exercise in which the students were invited to consider and, if they wished, to tell which of their own experiences they would like or not like to pass on.

Naturally groups of 20 or so would have very different concerns, but over the years the same few would crop up again and again:-

• Discipline – too harsh, too much or not enough.

• Freedom – not enough or too much.

• Television – ditto.

• Social life – encouraged or not.

• Bed times –too early or too late.

• Meal times – war or peace.

Between such recurring extremes, some middle-ground memories were considered more-or-less right. Just as often, though, that kind of golden mean was explicitly envied and recognised as the one to try and achieve.

I know that, for some in every class, this kind of airing and sharing was not easy: especially anything to do with the hidden messages. Often they are the ones that need both detachment and courage to confront, and I just hope those students were able to persevere with more time and privacy at home.

In your case there will be as much time as you need to pick and choose from your own experience the standards, values, methods and rules you want and do not want to keep.

It follows that the next step will be discussion with your partner to match, or at least compromise over what to select or reject. It is the sharing of these decisions that provides for consistency and the all-important united front, as your children will be quick to notice and take advantage of any gaps to play one of you off against the other. For single parents it may be very helpful to share your thoughts and memories with a sibling, other relative or trusted friend.

I hope by now you will have realised what all these memories and messages have to do with managing the behaviour of your children. I hope you will see how your choices and decisions are going to influence your expectations and demands.

And I especially hope you won't think all such picking and choosing would be an insult to your own parents. Instead, think of the old saying: 'the past is another country' with its different circumstances, possibilities, customs, attitudes and knowledge. Meanwhile social change, that used to be a gradual process, has been speeded up by media attention and discussion offering us quite different choices from those of our parents' generation.

Just think if our parents and theirs and all previous generations of parents had not learned the lessons of the past, we might still be having no fun on Sundays, still be repeating old stories about babies being born under gooseberry bushes and about masturbation causing blindness. We might still be sending our children up chimneys and down mines, and all keep in our house a buckle-belt, slipper or cane for the purpose of punishment.

While most of these horrors pre-date me by a good many years, my own 'generational experience' clearly makes the point.

My son Peter and his wife had plenty of time for this kind of consideration before the birth of their daughter, as well as plenty of ideas about the changes they were – or were not – going to make.

By then, though wincing a bit at one of two of their decisions, I had experience of two things that all grandparents would do well to keep in mind: -

1. Like the past, the future is also another country.
2. Unsolicited advice is rarely wanted or followed.

So recognising their very different circumstances and mostly holding my tongue, twelve years on, I am still as welcome in their house as they are in mine.

CHAPTER FIVE

YOUR TURN

By now I expect you can see how all this looking-back relates to the kind of parents you would like to be, and the kind of children you are would like to raise. So now it's your turn, with your partner or friend(s) to remember, to discuss and to <u>agree</u> what is worth – or not worth passing on.

TAKE WITH YOU	LEAVE BEHIND

I think this page would be useful to revisit from time to time for confirming, perhaps updating, or just proving the bright-eyed intent at which your more experienced selves may fondly smile.

CHAPTER SIX

RIGHT OR WRONG?

And now for the last exercise which my students found useful and sometimes even quite fun, so I hope the same for you.

At this point, everyone was asked to get to their feet and stand in the middle of the room where **YES** and **NO** printed cards were attached to opposite walls. They were invited to listen to a number of statements concerning the care of children, and to move towards the card which matched their own opinion. If unsure, it was suggested they take a position somewhere in between.

Here is a typical list from which three or four examples would be enough to make the intended point.

1. Children who don't eat their first course should not be allowed dessert.

2. Hitting children should be against the law.

3. Parents of young children should not divorce.

4. To be fair, all the family's children should be treated equally.

5. Body piercings (sometimes tattoos) are OK.

6. Children should keep their own rooms tidy.

7. Children should be allowed to stay up till they are ready for sleep.

But – I'm still _not_ ready to go to sleep!

8. Children should have pocket money.

9. Parents should always tell their children the truth.

10. TV in the children's bedroom is a good thing.

11. Parents should help teenagers to acquire contraceptives.

12. Young people should become accustomed to drink wine at home.

13. All school-age children should have cell phones.

By this stage of the evening it was easy to tell who in the group would be comfortable and confident enough to explain their position in the room. Then the rest were given the choice, if influenced, to move up or down.

Occasionally, when a simple explanation had missed some relevant point, I would step in to make it myself, often causing more movement in the room.

For example: from an elegant young woman firmly against body-piercing: -

Her: Because it's unhygienic, it looks tacky and probably going to leave a hole when they change their mind.

Me: I notice you have pierced ears for those nice drop-rings. How would you answer your teenager saying why not, if you do?

Her: Not ear rings of course; it's nose rings I mean, eye-brows, belly-buttons and those sort of studs in the tongue.

Me: So ear-rings are all right then?

Her: When they're old enough, probably yes.

Me: Age appropriate? Good answer, though there are cultural traditions in this country – maybe even in this room – of ear-piercing in babyhood. So what would be an appropriate age for you?

Her: High school? Graduation or something like that

Me: Nice idea, ear-rings for graduation, but what about all those other things?

Her: When they move out and get a job they can do what they want. Till then I won't be paying for their cigarettes or anything else I don't approve.

Me: Just sticking to your standards. Well said, well done and thank you very much.

*   *   *   *   *

Then, from a solemn man wearing a clerical collar, a perhaps predictable opinion about telling children the truth.

Him: Yes, about things that concern them I do think they should be told the truth.

Me: Like in court, the truth, the whole truth and nothing but the truth?

Him: Well yes to the truth and yes to nothing but; not so sure about the whole truth though. Some things aren't really suitable for young ears if you know what I mean.

Me: Yes, and you put your finger on it: things they're not ready for yet. I'm thinking of a disturbed thirteen year-old being told at a young age by his mother 'your father's in prison for fiddling with little boys' so you're going to have to watch it when he gets out.

Him: How tragic; poor child, what a terrible load.

That is an extreme example from my professional experience that of course has nothing to do with you but, like the vivid colours of a painter's 'broad brush', it does serve to make its important point.

My own relevant experience will seem much more likely to you. It was my second run through the 'facts of life' in response to five year old Peter asking 'mummy what is sex?' I didn't get much further than a man and a woman loving each other before his interruption: 'Oh I know, all that sperm and egg stuff. Anyway, Andrew's just got a guinea pig; can I have one too?' Funny rather than tragic, but also a good example of telling young children more than they want or need to know.

Another time, from a quiet, not-young man with a pony tail and peace-sign tee shirt, an unexpected 'No' to a law against hitting children.

Him: Because there's no way it could be enforced.

Me: Sounds, interesting; go on.

Him: Not without CCTV in all our houses, could it?

Me: You mean that's where it mostly happens?

Him: I don't know about that, but cameras all round the house . . .

Me: Not acceptable?

Him: Not to me anyway. I'd rather just trust my own and other parents' judgement and good sense.

Lots of nodding from the class and a lively debate about hitting: on the face, legs, bottom; with open hand, closed fist, hair brush, slipper – or not at all.

It was always this kind of follow-on discussion that got the students moving up and down, but still a typical result was a pretty even scatter all across the room. To some of them the 'intended point' was already clear, but to others it was relief to hear that there is no right or wrong about these – and many other – claims except what the parents, with their own shared convictions, decide.

More important than any difference between families is having, and keeping up, standards and values of your own.

Actually, when it comes to right and wrong in the care of children there are very few things – as the saying goes – written in stone. These are the ones that have been most important and useful to me.

1. All children need attachment to a consistent and attentive parent or carer.

2. Children learn through play: exploring their world, making believe, making a mess, acquiring new skills, learning by mistakes. **Rather than a waste of time, most play should be seen as children's 'work'.**

3. Self-esteem is both cause and effect of achievement, so make sure to notice and compliment your children for each – even small – success.

Once you have got the point of the 'Yes/No' exercise, you may think it really is one to skip with partners and friends, but discussing statements like these can still be useful to clarify your own thoughts and concerns, can reinforce or perhaps even change some of your decisions.

After all this thinking and deciding, here comes the easy part, as I used to tell my students: 'Nothing for you to do but relax and just listen'. In your case that means just relax and read on.

PART 3

CHAPTER SEVEN

HELPING CHILDREN TO BEHAVE

By now you have learned about the most common reasons for children's bad – and good – behaviour and, from your own childhood experience, have begun to consider your personal standards and priorities.

That was the hard bit with a lot to take in, so I can imagine you, like my students, thinking – some even saying – 'sounds like a whole lot easier said than done.'

My answer is that no one in their right mind would say raising children to be well-behaved is easy but, believe me, life is much harder when they're not, and many parents have been encouraged by the following suggestions; some even finding in them the best and most useful part of the course.

First a caution and a couple of reminders to help you off to a good start. It is no use just telling children to behave before the age when they can possibly know what that means. What you want them to do, or not to have done, needs to be clearly explained at the time, and usually more than once.

My first example of this is short and sweet. On being told to behave, my four year old granddaughter's wailing protest was: I am being have!

My second is of driving a little boy home along a country road after a play session at my house, and a conversation that went something like this:-

Him: Was I good today?

Me: Very important question. What do you think's going to be the right answer?

Him: I don't know.

Me: Well, let's think about all the things you did this afternoon.

Him: You mean like painting?

Me: Yes, your lovely colours for all those lorries and...?

Him: Tractors.

Me: Right, lorries and tractors; I think they're worth a toot on the horn, don't you?

Him: So it was a good picture?

Me: Yes, and so was the care you took mixing the paint, washing the brush between colours, keeping calm in the hard bits...

Him: Not spilling?

Me: Yes, not spilling - and cleaning up so nicely afterwards; that definitely deserves another toot.

There were three more toots to come: one each for feeding my cat, finding and putting on out-door clothes and carefully carrying his picture to the car. These he questioned, considered, counted and recounted before proudly announcing a total of six. In some of the following sessions he was able to better that score as he began to grasp what is meant by 'being good'.

Coming from a troubled and chaotic family, this seven year-old was seriously short of social skills and personal self-esteem. Your child will not have the same disadvantages, and you may not live near a road quiet enough for tooting (star charts, beans in a jar, achievement ladders would work just as well) but I think this story does serve to make the point about a child's understanding.

Just common sense, when you come to think of it, like most of the suggestions to come. But the trouble for many new parents is something, two things actually, even more common, which are:

1. Too little thinking time in trouble-spots and

2. In this age of experts, too little trust in their own good sense.

Your parents and grandparents may remember the encouraging words of their generation's child-care expert, Doctor Benjamin Spock: 'Trust yourself; you know more than you think you do.'

What you will see in the following pages is not a long list of one-size-fits-all rules; it is half a lifetime's worth of my – get it, my - suggestions to take or leave as you see fit

The first thing to keep in mind for any of them to work is **it's you the parents, and not the children who are in control.**

Who's in control has nothing to do with shouting the loudest or having the last word, at which, by the way, children are the real experts. Instead it has everything to do with having confidence in your own authority, with some good coping strategies up your sleeve.

That said, it is also useful to remember the second most common cause of children's misbehaviour: their need for more control over their own lives.

Doesn't that compromise, undermine or even contradict what I've just said about your own control? Not if you keep in mind it's for you, the parents, to decide which choices and freedoms to grant and when or when not to allow negotiation. What's more, if you have good reasons for second thoughts about your first decision, **there need be no loss of authority in changing your mind.** For example: postponing a premature or abused privilege is the right, even responsibility of every parent, and a good learning experience for any child.

And please don't feel guilty about being firm with your children, or worry about losing their love. Even perfect Penny had occasionally to reinforce her parental authority with snaps and growls which were heeded, but soon forgotten by the youngsters in her care. As long as you are fair, respectful and basically on their side, the same will happen with yours. So the third thing to remember before going on with the suggestions is that **tolerance of children's misbehaviour is no proof of parents' love; only of their weakness, uncertainty or exhaustion.**

I am sorry if you are giving up hope of ever getting to the 'best part', but this digression was necessary to make it, as has been claimed, also the 'most useful'. Well, here at last it is: with a whole lot of suggestions about, strategies for, and responses to, all seven causes of your children's unacceptable behaviour. You may find some I've specified for this or that need, actually more general purpose, so of course feel free to pick and choose.

Just as a particular pill relieves different kinds of pain, so several of the following 'remedies' are effective for different behaviour complaints. Therefore these you will find listed more than once.

1. GIVE ME MORE ATTENTION

It has already been said that round-the-clock attention is good for neither parent nor child, but most of the following suggestions will take only a few moments to carry out, and will have a much longer-lasting effect.

Make good behaviour worthwhile: notice, appreciate and even reward it, and take every opportunity to praise.

'A for effort' when it comes to bad habits which are rarely deliberate or easily cured all at once. For any improvement in things like swearing, slamming doors, leaving lights on or muddy footsteps on clean floors, your recognition and praise work much better than nagging or rage.

Take care to listen as well as explain.

Make a habit of reading to your children: In my line of work this is widely recognised as one of parent's most life-enhancing gifts. It is your time together with the comfort of closeness, as well as the actual story, that improves your children's vocabulary, and moral judgement, sparks their imagination, increases knowledge and understanding of their small world and kindles the curiosity and confidence to explore the wider worlds of school and beyond (just type 'reading to children' into your browser and you'll see).

> If you want your children to be intelligent, read them fairy tales. If you want them to be more intelligent, read them more fairy tales.
> —Albert Einstein

Of course not all read-to children will become 'straight A' students, models of propriety; rich, famous or specially talented, but this precious gift certainly gets them off to a good start, and helps them reach their own best goals.

Perhaps even more life-enhancing – anyway a real blessing & boon for children is the parents' daily example of their love and respect for each other.

Take photographs of your child's successes: (artistic, scholastic, athletic – even behavioural) to admire together from time to time, keeping in mind that **self-confidence is both cause and effect of achievement.**

Make time to watch some TV programmes together: from your attention and respectful discussion, you will probably learn more about your children than they will learn from you.

Play in and outdoor games together: As well as ticking your 'attention' box, games have much to teach about winning, losing, sharing, taking turns and team work that is a valuable preparation for real life.

Don't have all, or even most, meals in front of TV: neither meal nor programme gets full attention; food gets smeared or spilled and all the social advantages of sitting round the family table are missed.

Friends of mine with eight children used to have a second table for the demotion of those who were "boring" or badly behaved. If you have a big enough dining room, this might be worth a try, at least as regards behaviour. I'm not so sure about boring, but must admit that all eight, now grown up, are very good company at home, at work and at play.

2. GIVE ME MORE CONTROL OVER MY LIFE

Find or make opportunities to offer choices: better not too many at once; e.g. for encouragement: two different drinks, not six, or for a sanction 'You can go to bed right now or sit on the stairs all evening – your choice'.

Avoid false choices: like 'Do you want to come and have a bath?' or 'Bath time, OK?' unless any answer but yes is genuinely acceptable.

Give even very young children time and space . . . to explore, discover or just 'be'. According to child psychologist Lotte Bailyn: 'Instant availability without continuous presence is probably the best role a mother can play' (for 'mother' here, read parent or carer as well).

Encourage resilience and independence: With due regard to health and safety, be prepared to stand back and let your children make mistakes. They will learn more from getting things wrong than ever from adults showing or telling them what is right.

Start pocket money early: From the age of six or seven, a small weekly allowance gives the experience of decision-making, budgeting, even saving, and can be reduced or increased as either sanction or reward. It is also useful to test the conviction of children's 'must-have' pleas: with your offer to match, pound for pound, what they are able and willing to save. This equal-contribution disposes of one-day wonders, and releases you from their well-known pressure-power.

Make good use of your kitchen timer: Set the number of minutes you decide, or negotiate, for taking turns, sharing toys, measuring time out, or time till . . . bath, bed, story etc. This takes the heat off you, the 'mean parent' - especially if the child is allowed to set the timer him or herself.

Give a ten minute warning before play time must end: For play's end or workday's end, children as well as adults need wind-down time before packing up.

My most memorable experience of practising this particular 'preach' concerns another boy, this time a nine year-old cooped up in a small flat with his disabled mother, and clearly in need of some outdoor activity.

We had taken a wheelbarrow of supplies for a bonfire picnic in a nearby patch of riverside ground. After toasting and eating sausage sandwiches, he spent a happy hour on the shore, digging channels to let in water under and between bridges and fences he made out of twigs.

Just before packing up to go home, his protest at my ten minute warning was a wail of dismay and disbelief:

Him: Can't be, not already; I've only just started and you said at least an hour.

Me: I know, and I'm sorry, but that's what happens: time always flies when you're enjoying yourself; when you're having a good time'.

While I was re-loading the barrow, some indistinct but defiant muttering brought me to the bank where he was still arranging twigs around his channels and telling time – or some other power:

Him: Who says I'm enjoying myself when I'm not; not in the least, because this is no fun at all.

Took me a few moments to recognise his attempt to stop the clock, and the need, for a spoken count-down next time.

For toddlers, into everything, 'Not a toy' is useful code for 'Don't touch', saving more specific explanations which so often get you into the 'Why?' and 'Because' question and answer 'game'.

Three things you can't make young children do: sleep, eat and 'poo'. Promises, threats and nagging only add tension to these natural functions and may actually have the opposite effect. With relaxed encouragement and a few prompts and signals (things like quiet music or permissions to read in the bedroom; optional offers of unfamiliar food, and a potty or child-seat in the loo), in their own good time they will be able to manage for themselves.

Getting fussy eaters interested in food: involve them in making a menu, writing the shopping list and filling the supermarket trolley; then providing a 'proper' apron so they can help cook the chosen meal. Time hard for most parents to afford, but still well-spent in such a good cause.

> Less time-consuming, but also effective is the example of my friend preparing vegetables or fruit for the next meal. From these she cuts a few sections, slices or sticks onto a plate; put, without comment, on the table, chair or floor where her children are playing. Rarely does it come back to the kitchen with anything left.

3. I'M BORED. GIVE ME SOMETHING TO DO

Head off trouble at the pass with interesting or challenging things for your child to do, including the chance to let off steam in outdoor play, which often results in a good appetite, a calm evening and, at bed-time, readiness for sleep.

Outdoor activities for children of all ages and interests can be found online in the <u>Observer's Pocket</u> books and <u>Ladybird's Nature</u> series; also in the irresistible <u>Happy Holidays</u> by Alix Woods.

Keep a visible record of children's 'work in progress': their pride in each star on a chart, each bean in a jar, each sticker on the wall or step on a painted ladder is enough reward till some agreed and final treat.

In restaurants, to avoid children's boredom with slow service or adult conversation: bring along a word-search, sticker or colouring book (with crayons) to keep them occupied.

Most children like to cook: at least things they like to eat and, I've found, for extra fun, those which are normally brought ready-made. For example: bread, butter, peanut butter, jam, potato crisps, ketchup, mayonnaise can all be made at home, put in a store jar or packet to proudly 'trick' whichever parent will be coming home from work. Recipes for all these things can be found at the back of this book.

Some years ago an eight year-old boy came to my house every week for help with serious problems at home as well as school. He had been diagnosed with ADHD (attention deficit & hyperactive disorder) which sugar was supposed to aggravate, and I was asked not to give him any sweet snacks. He enjoyed making – and even more eating - sugar-free peanut butter, popcorn and potato crisps week after week. Then, on one of his bad school days, and one of mine lacking the right ingredients, we set about making some bread. At the kneading stage with a heap of dough on the table, I explained that stretching, squeezing and bashing it about was the best way to get it properly mixed. Soon he asked for something to 'make shapes', and chose from the nearby drawer a steak hammer, potato masher, rolling pin and a couple of wooden skewers. Louder than all the banging and bashing, was his stream of angry words: 'How many times to I have to tell you? Disgusting behaviour. Very, very bad. Bad boys have to get punished, don't they? Yes, they do. Do. DO!'

Leaving my dishes in the sink, I found he had flattened and shaped the dough into a face to poke and stab and beat with the rolling pin. Whoever it was being punished, justice was done, and he was able to roll it up again, and play some quiet games while it rose enough to bake, just in time: the perfectly smooth, round and still warm loaf – better than any smiley-face sticker - for him to take proudly home.

This was a hectic, impulsive, moody, curious, contrary, clever, sensitive, funny and sometimes charming child. I remember thinking he could be equally successful on the right or the wrong side of the law. Almost twenty years later, we are still in touch, and it is nice to know that he is on good terms with his family, has a girlfriend, a steady job and, now, plans to buy his own house.

Another extreme example of course, but your children will have their bad days and moods, and the calming effect of making bread is as well-known as its superior texture and taste.

Keep a 'treasure basket' full of small toys for the occasional treat or useful distraction. Restocked from time to time, it can give your own or visiting youngsters (from 18 months) a good hour discovering and rediscovering its contents, and allow you a welcome break.

Other items could be building blocks, ball-in-hole puzzles, Lego, stacking mugs, picture cards, cat bells, string of beads, magnets with paper clips or other bits of metal, unused spools of coloured thread, fir cones, Rubik's cube, a Russian doll with all its smaller selves inside.

The best value toy for children of all ages is a few stacks of paper cups from the pound store. With a little help even two or three year-olds can build a wall to be blown or knocked down with scrunched up newspaper balls.

And older children I know can keep going with one or more towers right up to the ceiling, and have equal fun throwing or blowing each other's down.

> **Plus points:**
> Good hand-eye coordination.
> Minimal cost.
> No risk of harm to people or property.
> No big deal if some get stepped on.
> When re-stacked very little storage space required.

4. CAN I GET AWAY WITH THIS?
(Testing boundaries)

Stick to just a few rules with consequences clearly explained; then a firm reminder of any that are broken can save a lot of argument at which most children can easily outlast you.

> When I was living in Canada, a friend's stroppy teenager came for some mutual respite to live with me. To avoid constant nagging, I found a common thread in her mother's many complaints, I lumped them all together under just one rule writ large on a card at the door of her room: PLEASE LEAVE EVERYTHING HOW AND WHERE YOU FOUND IT. I certainly can't claim instant success, but the finger of suspicion did get sopping towels picked up, spills wiped and the radio switched back from Kiss FM with no more objection than a weary sigh. Years later, and on the same principle, a small boy, pretending to be a swag-laden robber, did a very good job clearing up before leaving my house, so no one would even know he'd been there.

Ignore minor or harmless misbehaviour: like 'pulling a face', stamping a foot and just-audible rudeness: like petrol on smouldering embers, any reprimand risks escalation to a full-scale row, wasting time and attention better spent when your child is being 'good'.

Teach children the difference between 'important' and 'urgent': a good meal time conversation with your and their suggestions, like 'I can't find my hair brush' and 'Some thing's burning in the kitchen', as examples of when and when not to interrupt other's conversation.

Decide on a place for 'time-out': depending on the child's age, this could be a chair facing the wall, the bottom step of stairs, the hall or other area without interesting distractions; probably better not named the 'naughty' chair/step/place to avoid superstitious dread or mockery from others when in normal use.

For the same reasons (dread and mockery) you might not choose the bedroom but, for older children I have found 'reflection time' in their own room, till they are ready to come down, apologise or make amends, often works very well.

Abuse it and lose it works with privileges as well as toys and other possessions. A short 'sentence' – repeated if necessary – is usually more effective than a single long one which gives a child time to get interested in something else.

The same applies to time-out, especially for younger children. A good guide is one minute for each year of their age, or they get discouraged, bored or angry and likely to get into even more trouble. Usual time-out ground rules are: -

- You decide when.

- You decide where.

- You explain why and what are the rules.

- You do not negotiate.

• You ignore protest.

• You return 'escapers', resetting the clock as often as necessary.

• You check, when time's up, if the child remembers what it was for.

• You ask for an apology.

• You accept it with a cuddle or hug and agree to make a fresh start.

> If these rules are faithfully followed, children soon learn escaping doesn't pay, and least said is soonest mended so, new mothers, don't let such banishment break your heart.

For toddlers, into everything, 'Not a toy' is useful code for 'Don't touch', saving more specific explanations which so often get you into the 'Why?' and 'Because' question and answer game.

5. I'M CONFUSED, ANGRY OR FRIGHTENED
(And need your help and control)

For 'help me/control me' kind of behaviour: sometimes it is enough to sit quietly beside an angry or frightened child. There may be feelings to hear and acknowledge; or just holding may provide necessary protection and reassurance.

> This is not a good time to say 'you always…' or 'you never…' about your current complaint. This, like labelling the child, is more a weary prediction than encouragement to change. Better not said then or even at all.

Two moral questions for even quite young children to ask themselves:

'Would it be all right if everyone did this?'

'Would I like it if someone did it to me?'

Avoid boisterous play in the hour before bed: this is the time for a regular routine of quiet play, a last drink before bath, then story, a cuddle and a firm 'good night'.

Unless your child is not well, it is best to ignore protests and pleas, and return to bed, without discussion, any who come out of their room. If this is a new regime for you and your child it may have to be repeated several times before the penny drops. Parents are often advised the first time only to say something like 'It's time to go to sleep, darling; good night' and after that nothing while putting the child back in bed. Hard, I know, but children need their sleep and parents need time together for themselves. For how much is enough, see the sleep page in the Matters Arising chapter.

Food colouring in the bath water is a calmly enjoyable treat that doesn't upset the bedtime routine.

Birthday parties often end in tears, especially for younger children: from too much excitement, noise and food, as well as too many guests. A good number for a better result is one more than the age of the birthday child.

A good 'settle down' party game is the picture post card jig-saw puzzle. Several cards are cut (in two for toddlers, four or six for older children) and scattered, face up, on a table or carpet, each to be reassembled on a tray, hardcover book, or pre-cut square of cardboard.

6. JUST COPYING MY FRIENDS

A one-size-fits-all answer to this is some version of 'What your friends do in their house is their parents' business; what you – and they, for that matter, do here is ours'. As you read in the Yes/No exercise, there was no right or wrong about those – and many other - claims except what the parents, with their own shared convictions, decide.

> More important than any difference between families is having – and up-keeping – standards and values of your own.

7. WHY NOT IF YOU DO?

At such times the old excuse, 'Do as I say, not as I do', really won't wash: an honest own-up and apology will certainly be better given and received.

Example and precept: worry less that your children sometimes aren't listening to what you say, and more that they are always watching what you do.

> Children have never been very good at listening to their elders, but they never fail to imitate them.
> —James Baldwin

The best behaviour management strategy of all is your example of courtesy and respect.

CHAPTER EIGHT

ALL-PURPOSE SUGGESTIONS AND IDEAS

(Which recognise and demonstrate the wise old saying that prevention is better than cure)

Don't take 'being good' for granted: remember what you have already learned about the life-long value at such times of your attention and praise.

A different consequence is deserved for accidental and deliberate damage - even when the result is the same. Your recognition of this helps when it comes to owning up, and also allows for those faults due to immaturity or tempers not yet under control.

Punishing a child who has owned up to a misdeed is like whistling for a run-away dog and then hitting it, as it must seem, for coming back. At least credit the honesty with a lesser punishment, or allow him/her to say what it should be; you may be surprised how much tougher theirs, than yours would have been.

Teach children the difference between 'important' and 'urgent': a good meal time conversation with your and their suggestions, like 'I can't find my hair brush' and 'Some thing's burning in the kitchen', as examples of when and when not to interrupt other's conversation.

'No' often seems to be the two year-olds' favourite word. Who do you think they learnt it from? (Though to be fair, it is also a quite natural expression of their growing independence.) Anyway, try for yourself the effect of a conditional 'yes', as in 'Yes, but not right now', 'not today', 'not till xx (something the child should do) gets done', or at least 'I'll think about it', rather than an outright 'No'.

'I cut and you choose' helps fairness between two children sharing a cake.

With your own ideas, you probably won't need or take all these suggestions, but certainly there will be occasions when your and/or my 'preventions' won't succeed so now it is time to have a look at some usually effective 'cures'.

CHAPTER NINE:

DAMAGE CONTROL

'Give me a child till he is seven, and I will give you the man.' So the Jesuits have been saying, since the seventeenth century, about the young people in their care. The clear implication is that children don't suddenly become well-behaved the day after their seventh birthday. My own interpretation of this old saying is 'teach your child acceptable behaviour while s/he is still pick-up-able and carry-able to your choice of naughty, time-out or 'reflection' place in your home.

This point was well made for me in a confrontation with nine year-old, much-too-big-to-carry Peter about an uncompleted chore, when all I had to rely on was whatever respect he had by then for me and my moral authority.

Of course there will be some 'preventions' not at first successful or simply just missed. In the following pages, though, you will recognise quite a few of them repeated as equally, or even more, relevant at this stage.

Head off trouble at the pass with interesting or challenging things for your child to do, including the chance to let off steam in outdoor play, which often results in a good appetite, a calm evening and at bed-time, readiness for sleep.

Most DIY stores, and many carpenters, keep a bin for odds, ends, and off-cuts of wood, which, sanded down, can make unusual and innovative building blocks. Taking your child along engages the interest of both parties: one learning where the wood comes from; the other, where it's going to, more than likely declining your offer to pay.

Let your child know you recognise that the same thing done 'by accident' or 'on purpose' deserves a different consequence; helps when it comes to owning up; also allows for faults due to immaturity or loss of temper not yet under control.

Be ready with specific and all-purpose sanctions for unacceptable behaviour: for example, confiscation, grounding, time-out or even a period of your own 'non-cooperation'.

LABEL THE ACTION NOT THE CHILD. A much better remedy is the clearly made point that lying, cheating, stealing etc. will be punished and then forgiven for the chance of a clean sheet and a fresh start. Any reference to the child being in these and other ways bad, is unhelpful, unwise and all too likely to be self-fulfilling.

Reprimands which include 'you always...' and 'you never...' like self-fulfilling prophesies, come close to inviting or condoning more of the same.

'No' often seems to be the two year-olds' favourite word: Who do you think they learnt it from? (Though to be fair, it is also a quite natural expression of their growing independence.) Anyway, try for yourself the effect of a conditional 'yes', as in 'Yes, but not right now', 'not today', 'not till xx (something the child should do) gets done', or at least 'I'll think about it', rather than an outright 'No'.

Sarcasm is only, if ever, acceptable between equals in age and understanding.

An example I remember concerns an excited five year-old, too early up on Christmas morning, and his father, probably too late up the night before, now putting the kettle on in the kitchen. This is how the little boy's account of his wonderful stocking was interrupted in full flow.

Father: Thank you for wishing me a happy Christmas.

Son: Did I? I don't think so, I just . . .
Father: Exactly. You're right. You did not. What do you think is more important, manners or stockings, in this house?

Son: Um, but I just wanted to . . .

Father: Go to your room and think about it. Manners or stockings, NOW!

What a cloud to cast over that poor child's Christmas.

Don't give immature or unreliable children instructions you are too busy, tired or distracted to follow up. This only undermines your authority and invites the chancing of their arm another time.

Carrots are better than sticks for behaviour management. In the work place employers already know this, and in the home, wise parents will soon find out. So be ready with small, sometimes not so small, treats 'WHEN', not 'IF' this or that thing gets done. Two such little words with such big and different intent and meaning. To promise 'when' assumes compliance, while 'if', which at least allows for the right choice, is better kept for threats.

An early lesson for me was my 'if' failure to help a hefty, school-phobic thirteen year-old girl lose weight, compared to someone else's completely successful 'when'. I knew that her size was causing health as well as social problems at school; also that she was interested in ice skating – at least on TV. So my carrot for her, at our weekly sessions, was to walk together, each day a little further, up a nearby steep hill, marking her progress with a scrap of red wool tied in the hedge, and a trip to the skating rink **if** she reached the top. Week one: we made about 100 yards, week two, perhaps 125, and that was it. No more walking for this self-willed child, blaming the bad weather, the wrong shoes and other preferred activities.

As one of these was riding, which is known to be good exercise for both rider and horse, I made an appointment at a local stable. There she was very taken with a quiet and friendly horse, only to be told by the owner that she was too heavy, and to come back **when** she had lost at least a stone. Guess what? Three months later she was up in the saddle and well on her way to losing another.

This girl was with me for two more busy years before she was ready to move on. Then her 'graduation' celebration was that trip to the skating rink where she clung to me for a few tottering minutes at the edge, before letting go of my hand and — in both real and symbolic independence — pushed off to the far end all by herself.

Just one more word about 'carrots': they don't have to be expensive, dramatic or exciting treats; often a sweet or a coin for their money box is enough, or even 'we'll have lunch/TV/story when this or that thing gets done'.

It is no use arguing with angry or distressed children. They won't – probably can't – really listen: much better to allow a truce in different rooms until both parties are ready for a calm conversation.

Be ready with specific and all-purpose sanctions for unacceptable behaviour: for example, confiscation, grounding, time-out or even a period of your own 'non-cooperation'.

Abuse it and lose it works with privileges as well as with toys and other possessions. A short 'sentence', repeated if necessary, is usually more effective than a single long one giving a child time to get interested in something else.

To follow through with punishment chores, there is no loss of face for you encouraging or even helping a reluctant or flagging child.

All promises and threats must be followed through: and sooner rather than later, to earn your children's trust and respect.

Haven't we all heard – or even said ourselves – things like 'How many times do I have to tell you?' and 'I'm warning you, do that one more time and…?' Broken promises lose motivation, repeated threats just get ignored, and either, long awaited, are soon forgotten, like the one I heard in a supermarket on a sweltering <u>August</u> afternoon: a weary mother telling her troublesome four year-old 'Santa won't be coming to our house if your carry on like that.'

Sulking is a powerful weapon that should (excuse mixed metaphors) be nipped in the bud; not allowed to poison the atmosphere or pressure others to let the sulker have his/her own way. An effective bud-nip is 'please go and sulk somewhere else and come back when you are ready to talk.' Meanwhile it is worth considering what example is being followed here: is it the child's own experience that sulking works, or something learned from others at school – or even at home?

I know of a family where young children were used to their fallen-out parents communicating only through them, or with each other's written notes - for days on end. Yes, another extreme example, but one that does well make the point.

Whenever possible make punishment fit the crime: 'Clean up your own mess', 'that's coming out of your pocket money (replacement or repair), 'Return or replace the stolen item', 'If TV/I-Pad get in the way of homework, then no TV/I-Pad till that gets done' all have a logic that children can understand and respect.

Don't make confiscations last too long. A short 'sentence', repeated if necessary, is usually more effective than a single long one which gives a child time to get interested in something else.

Give a disgraced child a way out of trouble. Just as a rat will bite to get out of a corner, more trouble can be expected from a cornered child who may well respond to being asked, or advised, how to make amends. Especially don't let your child go to sleep in disgrace: if too late, too upset or too tired for a proper resolution, try a hug and promise to sort things out in the morning.

Children most need your love when they least deserve it. This does not mean accepting bad behaviour which may well justify an immediate sanction before a shared attempt to understand and address it. But, like many of my suggestions, it is love shown, not just told that will carry more weight with your children than any amount of absent-minded "love yous" as they come and go.

Don't expect gratitude, beyond well-taught thanks, from young children. Years of care, attention, discipline and love are indeed <u>your</u> gift, but also <u>their</u> birth right. Real gratitude comes later, with the perspective of time and experience – especially that of being parents themselves. Then you will be well repaid for all your loving care.

CHAPTER TEN:

CONCLUSION

If you are thinking all of this is a counsel of perfection, you are quite right. Of course there will be times when you lose your temper, when you are distracted, busy or just too tired to follow through with these suggestions. And there will be other times when your best efforts just aren't enough, but don't lose heart; children are very forgiving and you can always pick up the pieces and start again.

Meanwhile, instead of blaming yourself, just remember there is no such thing as a perfect parent. We all make mistakes with our children and regret things we have and have not done, but we can all take comfort from the teaching of one of our most respected child psychiatrists. Donald Winnicott claimed that even if perfect parenting were possible, it would not be in the best interest of children who need to learn, while still at home, how to deal with the failings of others as well as their own. With that in mind, all parents can – and need to – be is not perfect, but in Doctor Winnicott's time honoured expression, simply **'good enough'**.

So it only remains for me to wish you good luck, good health and happiness with your family in the years to come…

MATTERS ARISING

MATTERS ARISING

WHEN TO START BEHAVIOUR MANAGEMENT

In the first few months after birth, babies' 'behaviour' depends mostly on their digestion with its associated hunger and other discomforts. So what's to manage except input and output then?

I expect you have heard the description of a good baby as one who eats when fed, burps when patted on the back, sleeps when put down and while awake amuses itself playing with fingers and toes.

Lucky the parents of that baby, but what about the one who does none of these things: who fusses when fed, throws up when burped and, day after weary day, cries right around the clock?

Sounds like one I know whose father could hardly wait to get off to work in the morning and whose mother dissolved into grateful tears when asked by a friend, not if she was thrilled with her lovely new daughter, but if she was ready to throw her out of the window yet.

Is that one, and all other fractious babies, to be described as bad? Surely not if you think of their previous life experience in the warm, dark, quiet and constantly nourishing womb. Then compare this with the bright lights, variable temperature, loud noises, strange beds and only intermittent food in the outside world. Quite a shock to the system, I think you would agree, and perhaps even wonder whose is the greater challenge at this time. Is it the baby's, facing and adapting to all these uncomfortable changes? Or is it the parents', fitting in every day six milk feeds, three adult meals, shopping, housework, paper and paid work;

snatching a few hours of sleep whenever they can, with hardly a moment to share and take care of each other; when their only hope and goal is just getting by without their own tempers and tears?

I can't give you the answer; only suggest some small adjustments you can make to help yourselves and the baby through this difficult time.

The first one I learned, more than forty years ago, was from a cheerful doctor making his rounds in the hospital when I was 'rooming-in' with my new born son. Finding me tiptoeing around the sleeping cot, he practically roared, 'You don't want to spend the next few years creeping round like that, lassie. Right from the start our kids slept through my bagpipes. Babies'll sleep through a lot worse, believe you me'.

Neither I nor anyone else I know plays the bagpipes, but I did find the same applied to kitchen clatter and other normal household noises as well.

Before or soon after the birth you will have had your reasons and made your choice about feeding. It may be breast, bottle or some combination of the two, considering either or both parents' employment, and the chance for some nice bottle-bonding with dad. Millions of babies have been successfully raised with any of these options, so none need be the cause of regret, guilt or shame.

Having difficulties with breast-feeding, my daughter-in-law soon switched to bottled milk with this innovative method:-

1. Buy a set of feeding bottles with disposable liners.

2. Keep a 24-pack of bottled water in the kitchen.

3. Just before each meal, make up the required amount.

4. Safe to 'serve' at room temperature whenever and wherever needed, without the kit and caboodle of sterilization, just a fresh water bottle each day.

While she recommends anyone tempted to follow suit first to check with their health visitor, I can assure you the change was a relief to all concerned, especially the increasingly happy, healthy and well-fed child.

Over the last century, fashions in baby care have come and gone and come back again. The range has been from a strict 'feed, burp, change, put down and ignore all crying' regime, to the 'baby-sling, demand-feed, share-a-bed, always in touch mother-earth' routine. Other, less extreme, models include behaviour management which responds to babies' needs while encouraging them to fit in with – rather than dominate – family life.

In any case, though, all babies do need burping, and most of them have preferences for after-food comfort: face up or down on the lap, heart-to-heart, over the shoulder, rubbing, rocking or just walking around, which you will soon discover for yourselves, and find worth the extra few minutes they take. None of this special attention amounts to actual 'management', but it may well be the foundation of your baby's secure attachment and confidence in your relationship.

As this is soon to be tested in your sleeping arrangements, I do recommend some real behaviour management right from the start. Although sleep is one of the natural functions that can't be controlled, there are some things you can do to help your baby, and yourselves, to get enough. For these please see the following pages on Bed Time.

When it comes to toddlers, much good and bad behaviour depends on safe-proofing their environment. This is mostly a matter of putting forbidden things out of reach and arranging meal and bed times to avoid hunger, tiredness and temper.

Parents' approval and disapproval are obvious to most small children and usually motivate their behaviour without any more need for sanction or reward than frequent cuddles or a few minutes of time out. More specific, spelled-out discipline can wait until they are old enough to understand instructions and rules. Many of the suggestions in previous chapters apply to this stage and need not be repeated here.

Even so, there is more to be learned from TV parenting programmes like The House of Tiny Tearaways, Super Nanny, Three-day Nanny and Nanny 911, including when behaviour management should begin. Without being actually spelled out, it is pretty obvious from its absence in struggling families from all walks of life.

In case you haven't had the chance to see any of these programmes, and since their message matches my own, here it is, loud and clear:

When to begin behaviour management? The sooner the better, and best of all, right from the start.

DUMMY OR THUMB?

Have you ever wondered why such an unkind, even disdainful name was given to the most popular little mother's helper ever known?

Dummy: the very word suggests a false substitute for the real thing, meaning in this case, of course, the nipple of a bottle or breast.

This name was in use throughout my childhood when stay-at-home mothers could feed their babies around the clock, and the well-to-do had nannies to cope with those who fretted and fussed.

Meanwhile, and mostly in America, more accurate, apt and friendly names, like 'pacifier', 'soother' and 'binkie', have taken over, perhaps in sympathy with the different circumstances of most mothers today.

Even so, many parents-to-be who vowed they never would, soon find themselves utterly dependant on this little faker to get them through the day, and often also the night.

Well, there is no question that babies like and need to suck, and without a dummy, the most handy thing (literally) is going to be the thumb, especially as prenatal scans have shown foetus thumbs in the mouth as early as the 15th week.

So, dummy or thumb: which is it going to be in your house? Here are a few pros and cons to both that may help you to decide.

Dummies can be relied on to soothe or pacify the normal grumps and gripes of most babies any time of day or night: especially useful in public or the company of adult friends. Oral myologist (finder, fixer and writer about mouth problems) Rosemary Van Norman, claims the natural endorphins produced by thumb-sucking can just as well serve the same purpose. As other experts point out it's the sucking, not what's sucked, that produces the endorphins, it's Even Stevens so far.

Dummies get dirty from being thrown on the ground. So do thumbs, once babies begin to crawl.

Thumbs are always available, dummies sometimes are not.

Dummies lost during the day, parents can find or replace; not so easy for a wakeful baby to find one lost in the cot at night.

A dummy in the mouth gets in the way of a baby's babbling which is the necessary precursor of speech. A thumb in the mouth gets in the way of any 'learning through play' that involves the use of both hands.

Dummies and thumbs have both been blamed for misshapen or prominent teeth. You'll be glad to hear the expert opinion that neither affects the first (milk) teeth, though both should be stopped before the second (adult) teeth grow in. These are the ones that could be affected and require braces or even surgery later on.

So, how and when to start the stopping? Energetic, curious, confident children may gradually give up the thumb in order to play, just as the talkative, sociable ones may voluntarily spend more time without a dummy in their mouth. If not, parents should encourage at least day-time abstinence in time to avoid teasing and embarrassment in nursery or reception class at school.

A nice way with dummies is to arrange a little ceremony for giving them back to the dummy fairy who needs them for other babies and will replace them with a more 'grown-up' present instead. As for thumbs, perhaps a cute thumb ring as both reminder and reward, or – but only if your child is willing – a pretty 'thumb glove' may also do the trick. *See* References and Resources, page 206.

Anyway, you can see the 'expert' case for dummy or thumb, at least up to toddler stage, is pretty evenly balanced, so after all, your choice may come down to something as trivial as whether you do or don't mind the appearance of a dummy in your child's mouth.

BED TIME

Why, in so many families, is this far from the peaceful time that, right from the start it can, and ought to be? After all there's no question that one way or another, <u>all</u> babies will eventually fall asleep. For the sake of peace, though, there is more than one answer as to the how, the where, and the when.

While working in a Canadian hospital I came across a young Native American woman on the obstetrics ward, admitted for the last month of her pregnancy because of a blood pressure problem. Pitifully homesick in this unfamiliar place, she found some comfort in talking to me about her far-off family and friends. Then, after the safe delivery of her son, I was able to take up an invitation to visit her tiny house on the reservation.

She came to the door with the baby in a neat bundle, sound asleep on her back. A native custom, she said, for combining child-care with work and social activities. After some strange-tasting tea she showed me how the bundle was made from a large triangular shawl draped over the baby's shoulders, with two corners crossing her chest, taken round the back and securely tied with the third corner under his little behind. Then she showed me how she kept him close at night in an, also home-made, hammock by the bed where she could reach out when he woke and rock him back to sleep.

Pregnant myself at the time, I was charmed by these simple arrangements, later copying and finding very useful the hands-free baby back-pack.* The hammock, though well suited to this mother's way of life, was not to mine with a doctor-in-training husband needing his own quiet sleep while I came and went to feed the baby in another room.

*For proof of the security of the back-pack see the photograph at the front of the book.

That was my how, where and when, more than forty years before the publication of 'The Sensational Baby Sleep Plan.' In this book, renowned sleep expert Alison Scott-Wright gives a lot of sensible advice based on her experience that all healthy babies, from the age of twelve weeks, are capable of sleeping right through the night! That's my exclamation mark, as one of many mothers who were and still are prepared for 2.00, 6.00, 10.00, 2.00, 6.00, 10.00 feeds round the clock, as well as wakeful periods in between.

I know some parents accept this as a normal, natural, even pleasurable routine; while others just grin and bear, abandoning hope of the chance to enjoy both baby and grown up time together with their friends.

Whatever your preference, the advice of Mrs. Wright, of many child psychologists, and all the TV nannies, seems to me a reasonable compromise between the extremes of ever-present mother-earth and feed-burp-leave-to-cry practice. In that case your baby's good sleeping habits are going to depend on a consistent, well-established routine.

Here is one that starts in the early evening, takes no more than an hour, and nicely addresses both your own and your baby's needs. It works best with no day time nap after 3.30 pm, and no excitement, just calm play in the last hour before, around 6.30, heading off for a 15 minute bath. Once in bed, there is still time for some quiet chat, songs, back rubs and cuddles before you leave the room. Staying till the baby falls asleep is a workable option as long as it involves no more engaging 'conversation'.

A word of warning about this option: the longer it continues, the harder it is for the child to give it up. I even know of a twelve year old girl unable to fall asleep without her mother beside her on the bed.

The guiding principle here is that infant sleeping 'behaviour' is not instinctive, but learned from parents' response to their baby's signals. If you follow the routine, as recommended, from his or her 12th week, that lesson is soon and easily learned.

A later start will take longer. Babies who habitually wake in the night may have already learned that crying gets them a cuddle or a nice warm drink. In that case their new lesson is to expect no more than a brief visit from one or other parent, with a quiet reminder that it is time to sleep; no picking up, no cuddles, no conversation and just a sip of water – or even nothing more to drink.

Either way, and of course, for prolonged or frequent crying, you need to consider special reasons like too much or too late day-time sleep, too little or too early day-time food; teething, colic or acid reflux which might need the extra help of your health visitor or GP.

You may have heard of young children who can't sleep without a light in their room because they are afraid of the dark. How come, I wonder, after nine months safely spent in the dark of their mother's womb? As most adults sleep better with curtains drawn and no light on in the room, wouldn't the same be true for children as well? I don't know for certain, but my instinct is that it would allow them better sleep and avoid unreasonable fear of the dark.

The only scientific claim I've found on this subject was in a BBC report (12th May 1999), of some incomplete

American research connecting children's short sightedness with sleeping in a lighted room. That was refuted by specialists at Moorfields (London's famous eye hospital) saying the condition is more likely to be inherited from either or both parents, and that low-level lighting in children's rooms will do them no harm.

Update: According to Dr. Mario Motta (AMA Council of Science and Public Health), 'Exposure to light at night disrupts the production of melatonin which is made during sleep . . . [and] is thought to be a cancer suppressor, [and] that exposure to light may accelerate the development of cancer.'

It was not this risk, however, but that of possible weight gain, which finally determined my 13 year-old granddaughter to sleep in the dark.

While waiting for more research on these and other possible risks, Dr. Motta's advice to parents is for their children to go to bed at the same time every night, with no more light in the room than a dim red bulb for any who are afraid of the dark.

Anyway, whatever your decision about lighting, babies' bedtime routine needs only a few adjustments when they reach the toddler stage. Things like longer play downstairs or in the bath, last drink, last wee, last story from a chosen book; then the familiar settle-down and firm 'good night'. After that the same response to wakeful crying is recommended though, at this age, nightmares are not uncommon and belong on the list of 'special reasons' for extra comfort to be checked out.

When it comes to graduation from cot to bed, most toddlers see and take the opportunity for escape: to come downstairs in the evening, or later on into your own bed. The best time for such family togetherness is on a lazy weekend morning, not in the middle of a week-day night. This bid for attention, like the baby's night time crying, should be similarly discouraged if you're not going to become like those distraught families on a TV Nanny show.

I know that many school-age children have a television in their bedroom which they are allowed to watch until they fall asleep. While this assures peace and quiet for the parents, here are some things to consider before encouraging a habit that will be hard to break.

1. Most children have already had enough screen time on their phones and I-pads during the day.

2. Children often find themselves in bedrooms away from home where TV is not available or allowed, and should not depend on it to be able to fall asleep.

3. Without parents' supervision, they are able and quite likely to be watching things you would prefer they did not.

4. Even if you have managed to block all unsuitable programmes, a far better habit for this down-time is one started with bed-time stories long ago. Given the well-known advantages of reading, surely it is preferable for your child to nod-off over the plot of a favourite book, than the flickering images of night-time TV.

In April 2012, *The Daily Telegraph* quoted Jan Turner from The Sleep Council that, "Two thirds of our children are not getting enough sleep."

After the when and the where, comes the how, as in how much sleep do children need? A 2012 poll by Travel Lodge showed the average six year old goes to sleep at 9.33 pm;

eight year olds at 9.49 pm, and 15 + not till 11.52. That was followed by the National Sleep Council survey in 250 primary schools which found that 'lack of sleep is having a devastating effect in schools with nine out of 10 teachers complaining that pupils are so tired they are unable to pay attention in class'.

Clearly not all right; so how much sleep is enough? The hours recommended by the National Health Service for different age children are listed on the following page for your guidance while your own are growing up.

Meanwhile, for those parents who didn't follow or succeed with their bed-time routine, it is never too late to make a fresh start. Old lessons can be replaced by new ones at any age. Bed times can be imperceptibly brought forward by 15 minutes a week, night time vigils abbreviated, bright lights gradually reduced with a dimmer switch and nice warm drinks replaced by just a sip of water, till there is no longer any reward in staying awake.

The point of my persistence here is that enough sound sleep is your and your child's best preparation to tackle life's inevitable challenges and problems.

HOW MUCH SLEEP DO CHILDREN NEED?

There are no hard and fast rules about the exact number of hours sleep children of different ages need, but the NHS offers some broad recommendations developed by the private Millpond Children's Sleep Clinic.

1 - 4 weeks: $15\frac{1}{2}$ – $16\frac{1}{2}$ hours per day, typically in short periods of 2 – 4 hours. (Premature babies may sleep for longer, and colicky ones for shorter periods.)

3 months old: 15 hours per day. (Developing regular patterns)

6 months old: 14 hours per day. (Often a good time to drop one of the usual three day time naps, as by now they are quite capable of sleeping through the night).

9 months old: 14 hours a day. (From here on the ratio of day to night time sleep moves towards 11¼ hours at night and 2¾ hours in the day.)

1 year old: 14 hours a day. (Morning nap usually given up, leaving the day: night sleep ratio at 2½: 11½ hours.

3 years old: 12 hours a day. (At this age, the 11 hours between typical bed times, 7.00 – 9.00 pm, and wake ups, 6.00 – 8. 00 am; that leaves 1 hour for the afternoon nap.)

4 years old: 11½ hours a day (Reasonable to expect with, by now, no day-time naps).

5-12 years old: 11½ hours a night.

12-16 years old: 8½–9¼ hours per night.

MASTURBATION

(OED definition: Stimulation of the genitals for sexual pleasure)

Believe it or not, like it or not, remember it or not, this is something that, at least in early childhood, we all, both girls and boys, have done. And yes, infants do have sexual feelings that are not associated with lust, which of course comes later on.

Right from the start it is through the five senses that babies explore and discover things about their world and themselves. No doubt it is the sense of touch that acquaints them with their genitals as an ever-ready source of pleasure and comfort which they may resort to, for either or both, for years to come.

It is most common in children between the age of two and five, or perhaps just more noticeable before they have learned from their parents to be more discreet. In either case it usually becomes less frequent, or at least less obvious after the age of five.

If this behaviour is going to embarrass or even worry you, here are some facts and 'expert' advice which may help you find a comfortable balance between your feelings and those of your child.

Occasional masturbation is normal for toddlers and pre-schoolers, particularly when they are tired, bored or distressed. It is not an illness. It causes no physical harm. It does not mean your child will become over-sexed, promiscuous or sexually deviant.

Not long before retiring, I came across a misguided father who was concerned about the masturbation of his 18 month-old son. More than concerned, I found him actually distressed at the thought that it might cause the child to become a homosexual 'wimp'. His solution for the unsupervised night time was for his wife to put the boy's all-in-one sleep suit on backwards so the front opening was out of reach.

I showed him a photograph of two year-old Peter, sitting on a tricycle with a thumb in his mouth, a hand down the front of his pants and a dreamy, contented expression on his face. Then another of him at age 18, receiving an award from the Duke of Edinburgh for joining an ecological expedition to the North Pole, and a third showing his over-head karate kick that was part of an upcoming black-belt test.

Of course there are homosexual men and women who have been on expeditions to the North Pole, and/or achieved black belt status in the martial arts. His son may well turn out to be one of the estimated 10% of men who are homosexual, but this would have nothing to do with childhood masturbation. It was the first step-change for this family which I know my colleagues continued to support with the same kind of advice given here by Doctor BD Schmitt of the American Academy of Paediatrics.

1. It is impossible entirely to eliminate masturbation; parents' disapproval or punishment, by increasing the child's need for this kind of self-comfort, is likely to have the opposite effect.

2.   On the other hand, completely ignoring all masturbation does no favour to the child who needs to know in what situations it could bring embarrassment to others and shame to him or herself. Sounds like the rock or the hard place, doesn't it?

3. The only, and possibly most helpful, thing you can do is to stand firm on the matter of where and when. Once the child is old enough to understand, an explanation that 'private parts' are best kept private will justify your limiting masturbation to the bath, the bed or some other private time and place.

4.   Meanwhile for toddlers, the same distractions and diversions suggested for tantrums on page 106 may be immediately effective, and eventually convey your preference without any hint of shame or blame.

5.   Some children masturbate less if they get plenty of hugs and cuddles; ideally at least a daily hour of affectionate attention from their parents or carers.

6. Although masturbation is known to cause no physical harm, the emotional harm of guilt and sexual hang-ups is likely to be caused by parents' overreaction, especially any suggestion that it is a dirty or wicked thing to do.

> "Feelings of shame, anxiety, inhibition, guilt, or remorse, may lead to [the child's] arrested sexual development, leaving him or her unable to achieve appropriate [adult] relationships involving trust, closeness, and positive sexual expression." —Caroline Rosdahl and Mary Kowalski, The Textbook of Basic Nursing.

7. For a child still masturbating when s/he starts day care or school, it's helpful to discuss your attitude and strategies with the care staff or teacher, and maybe also learn something from theirs.

If, after all your best efforts, you are worried about little or even no progress, you may need the professional help or your health visitor or GP.

For more information, visit:
www.nhs.uk/chq/Pages/1684.aspx?

Meanwhile, you won't have missed the point of all that information and advice: that it's a calm, confident and uncritical attitude towards masturbation which best helps your child to self-regulate this normal and harmless behaviour. For some parents it will be quite a challenge, and for some children it will take longer than others to reach the goal that will free you all up to concentrate on more interesting things.

BITING

Many parents I know are more troubled by this than any other kind of childish aggression. Their first and reasonable concern is for the actual risk of injury and the possible risk of infection. That is usually followed by some expression of distaste, or even disgust, for such 'primitive behaviour'.

According to my dictionary primitive behaviour 'occurs in early or very early stages of growth in response to unconscious needs and desires [and is] not affected by objective reasoning'. Sounds like a good match for the usual age of biting, when that kind of reasoning is the last thing parents can, or should, expect.

By this standard and at this stage, biting is not morally or socially worse than kicking, spitting or hitting, and deserves no more from parents than their same calm and firm response to all other greedy, spiteful and selfish acts of aggression.

Sometimes, though, there are more innocent reasons for biting, such as the need, when hungry or teething, for something to nibble and chew, or with pre-verbal children it may be an expression of feelings they can't yet explain: like out-of-control excitement, impatience for some expected attention, toy or treat; imitation or justified resentment of the behaviour of another child.

Also, remember that babies' first test of interesting things is by mouth: starting with the nipple of breast or bottle, parents fingers and offered toys. Once crawling, these will include pretty well any small object they find on the floor. At this stage they need guidance about what is and is not OK to bite.

With so many possible causes, even the most watchful parent won't always be able to anticipate or recognise the reason for an upcoming or actual bite. So, for your guidance here is some reassuring information and good, all-purpose advice.

From our NHS: Biting is normal behavior in young children and no sign of a particularly aggressive personality.

Though infection from saliva is rare and seldom serious, if the skin is broken, seek medical advice just in case.

Signs of infection include:

Redness & swelling around the wound
Associated heat and/or pain
Leaking liquid or pus
Temperature of 38C/100.4F
Sweats and chills
Swollen glands under chin, in neck, armpits or groin.
Red streaks on skin around the wound.

First Aid:

If skin is broken, encourage slight bleeding with gentle pressure on each side.

Run a couple of minutes under warm tap water to clean.

Cover with clean dressing and don't wait for symptoms of infection before seeking medical advice.

And from the Canadian Paediatric Association: Most bites are harmless and don't even break the skin. Those that do are seldom deep enough to draw blood.

Even so, infection is rare because 'fortunately spit is swimming in antibodies that reduce the infectiousness of bacteria in their midst'.

If either biting or bitten child is known to have hepatitis B, a doctor should be consulted as this can be transmitted by a bite to or from each one.

Hepatitis C is very rare in young children and no infection from biting has ever been reported – nor, for that matter, from HIV.

If the skin is not broken, clean the area with soapy water, apply a cold compress and comfort the child. If it is, don't squeeze the wound, just apply a mild antiseptic, plaster or bandage and watch a day or two for redness or swelling which should be seen by a doctor.

That's all the necessary first aid, but parents still need to work on strategies for prevention and cure of the tendency to bite. For this, the step-by-step advice of most child-care professionals fits well with the principle and practices of my class, and I hope also with your own.

After first separating the children, your immediate care, rightly given to the bitten one is, for the biter, a small but important lesson that this behaviour doesn't deserve, or get, your instant attention. That may come second, third or fourth after things like notifying the other parent, contacting the doctor or just time for you to think how best to deal with the biting child.

Shouting or harsh punishment will not reduce biting; more likely, by increasing the original confusion, resentment or anger, it will have the opposite effect.

Much better would be, and this is the best time for, teaching your child the social skills to deal with those troublesome feelings him/herself. For example: 'Please don't bite, Jack/Jill. Even if you're angry or out-of-sorts, biting hurts and it's always a bad thing to do to another person. I know you were fed up with Ben taking so long on the swing, but let's find another way of sorting that out so you two can both apologise, shake hands and get back to being friends.' This is not likely to be an instant cure, but once explained like this, brief periods of time out certainly are justified for any re-offense.

Ignore kitchen-table/coffee-morning advice from friends about biting back to teach your child a lesson. Think about it: you wouldn't want to bite hard enough to leave a mark, and a token nip makes no physical impression, just the mental one that it's all right for adults but not for children to bite. The only lesson that may be worth a try is to ask your child to bite his/her own hand: hard or soft, there could be something learned from that.

Don't start off on the wrong foot by laughing, or letting anyone else laugh when your child gives you an experimental nip. It's never too early to learn from a calm but firm response that biting another person is not acceptable behaviour.

After all these Don'ts here are some tried, true and effective Do's.

1. Notice what's been happening before a bite, such as a delayed meal or bed time, preparation for a play-date or the emergence of a new tooth. Have a few trouble-busters up your sleeve, like rusks or carrot sticks for teething and

hunger; a cuddle, dummy or early bath for fatigue; a home-made welcome poster with crayons for colouring in.

2. Sharing toys is the most common trigger for biting which can usually be avoided with the use of a kitchen timer for taking turns.

3. If, at home or day care, the same child is either biting or bitten, it's a good idea to have a no-blame discussion with the other parent or care staff for the exchange of strategies that will provide both children with your consistent and united front.

4. Right from the start make conversation with your children. Even while it's you doing most of the talking, they are sponging up words, meanings and sentence structure until they are ready to join in. Then it's your patient listening that encourages their verbal expression of the feelings that so often underlie biting and other aggressive behaviour.

5. Back up your efforts with a bed time story book on this subject. In 'No Biting' by Karen Katz and 'Teeth are not for Biting' by Elizabeth Verdick you'll find engaging text and amusing illustrations as well as some useful management tips.

6. Not all of you will need all of this advice as not all children are persistent biters. Those who are usually grow out of it around the age of four when they have learned better, more 'civilised' forms of self-expression. For those who have not, your GP may find a related health problem, or else make a referral for some professional counselling.

TANTRUMS

The National Health Service advises that temper tantrums may start as early as 18 months and are very common by the age of two (no doubt contributing to that 'terrible twos' reputation), and gives as cause the frustration felt by toddlers unable verbally to express their feelings, fears, wants and needs.

According to clinical psychologist Ray Lacy, for children in general 'every single tantrum results from one simple thing: not getting what they want' and for 1-2 year olds in particular, 'from trying to communicate a want or need without the [necessary] language skills.'

This explanation is widely accepted by child care professionals, with the NHS including, also, less selfish causes, like tiredness, hunger, jealousy and other emotional distress.

When Peter was a toddler, two hours was long enough for a play-date, sharing toys and my attention with a friend's daughter about the same age: long enough for both, and a delayed pick-up call was not good news for either one.

To comfort the anxious little girl on my lap, I reached for a soft toy which Peter immediately snatched back and hugged defiantly to his chest. Coaxing, reprimands and reassurance had no effect on the one, scowling, and the other, now tearful, child.

At that time I had no experience of tantrums but, looking back, I can see at least one, maybe two, well on the way. Luckily we were saved, literally by the bell and tearful one's mother at the door.

> Post mortem with scowler:
>
> His part: 'That was my best toy'. 'Well she's not my friend any more'. 'Because you like her better than me'. 'You're much nicer to her, that's why'.
>
> My part: Explanation of jealousy (a new word for his vocabulary) and promise to respect a whispered SOS whenever he feels it coming on.
>
> Result: A wiser mum, a happier little boy, more and better play-dates and, as far as I remember, a concession not over-used.

For my students, tantrums were always, and often first, on the list of dreaded behaviour, so for you all, with the when and the why out of the way, now comes the what, as in 'what's the best way to cope with them?'

As usual with behaviour problems, prevention is better than cure, and here are some suggestions for heading trouble off at the pass.

For a start, there is evidence that quick-tempered parents often have quick-tempered children, so the deep-breath-and-count-to-ten tactic, useful to all parents facing a tantrum, is especially recommended for those with a naturally short fuse.

There is a known relationship between children's language skills and the incidence of tantrums: i.e. the more of the one the less of the other. As the average two year-old's vocabulary has only fifty words, it makes sense to talk lots, not just to, but also **with** your child: to recognise and label some of those feelings, fears, wants and needs, so they can be expressed in words instead of rage.

'If you're happy and you know it clap your hands'. From day care or children's TV, most toddlers will be familiar with this song which you could adapt with agreed signals for other emotions like sorrow, anger, hunger and fear. This and all follow-up discussion would further increase language skills, should decrease tantrums and will demonstrate your on-side understanding and help your child's own self-control.

Meanwhile be prepared for typical tantrum times; not necessarily the same for all children, but getting dressed to go out, getting or not-yet getting fed, having to share toys, to finish playing or get ready for bed are common melt-down times which may or may not match your own.

For others, which seem to come out of the blue, there <u>are</u> usually warning signs and you will soon come to recognise things like whining, scowling, throwing objects and other attention-seeking behaviour which a quick food/fear/fatigue check and response may nip in the bud.

If not, as toddlers are naturally curious, you could try a cheerful distraction like 'Goodness, what's that outside the window, let's go and have a look', or a diversion to some enjoyable activity like drawing a picture, reading a story or, because a change of venue often works, taking a swing in the garden, bread for the birds, or what's anyway needed, a walk with the dog.

If still not, a full-blown tantrum may yet be avoided by something like this <u>calm</u> response to your angry/sulking/sobbing child: 'If that's what you want to do, I'll just sit here/be in the kitchen till you're done'. It's important to be in sight, or at least earshot at the time in case of breath-holding, choking or other harm. That 'calm' is underlined because your composure is a good example and reassurance to a truly troubled child and an appropriate denial to one who just wants his or her own way.

Any attempt at diversion with mockery, teasing or tickling is an inappropriate denial of genuine feelings and more likely to fuel, than defuse an oncoming tantrum. Anger and frustration that doesn't come out doesn't just go away; it stays in with more or different trouble to come.

I'm thinking of that little boy making bread, and further back to Peter's knock-down-and-bounce-back doll: a splendid, stereotype enemy that could legitimately, and most satisfyingly, be punched and kicked. These can still be found on the internet in a variety of guises and, on Amazon under Therapeutic Bop Bag, a featureless one with a set of washable markers for a child's own choice and use.

Tantrums due to a request refused may be headed off by a conditional 'yes' instead of an outright 'no'; for example 'Yes when you've picked up those crayons', 'Yes when you've apologised to x', or 'Yes when you've sat quietly for five (kitchen timer) minutes with your book'. If your child follows through, there's a good lesson learned: if not, don't change your mind; tantrum or no tantrum, giving-in is a lesson you don't want to teach.

*   *   *   *   *

From here on, keep in mind what you've already learned about behaviour management: about attention for the good, no pay-off for the bad, in either case labelling the action not the child; time out, and especially remember the class message of tantrums: **I'm confused, angry or frightened and need your help and control.**

Now here, to help you, is some useful information and advice from the National Health Service, other child care professionals and from my own experience.

A genuine tantrum is not deliberate; it is out of control behaviour that's much more distressing for the child than it need be for you. That 'genuine' is to distinguish the real from the fake of a child who has already learned that tantrums pay off. Not always easy to recognise, but you could try calling a suspected bluff, as in 'if you think that's going to get you xyz, you've got the wrong idea; xyz is for children who are at least trying to behave. If that, and brief period of time out doesn't work, consider and proceed as for 'real'.

In either case, this is not time for a yelling match (which anyway you are unlikely to win), nor blame, threats or punishment of any kind. So, try to stay calm and keep your voice down while putting sharp and dangerous objects out of harm's way.

In mid- tantrum, it's no use lecturing, reasoning or asking for explanations; at this stage, psychologists have found, 'the rational part of the brain is switched off'.

It may help turn battle-ground into field-hospital to sit on the floor (or same level) and quietly acknowledge the known or suspected problem: for example 'I know it makes you angry/frightened/jealous/if such-and-so, and when you feel better, let's see if we can sort it out together so it won't happen again'.

Of course, not all tantrums occur at home. Play grounds, supermarkets and restaurants are all danger zones for which you can be prepared with things like:

1. A kitchen timer for a 10 minute warning of time to go home (and also useful for end of play and time before bed).

2. A mini shopping trolley and list of items to choose from and find.

3. A sticker or colouring book with crayons.

If not successful, for everyone's sake, permanently or temporarily remove a kicking and screaming child to another room or the strap-in seat of the car. No need to feel embarrassed; on-lookers will have good reason, not to scorn, but to admire your calm and firm response.

Indoors or out, once the storm is over, parents and exhausted child may be in need of some down-time (nap, bath, TV) before a sympathetic discussion of causes and, for the future, better preventions and cures.

All this is asking a lot of busy parents with jobs, partners and other children to take care of as well, and I expect you'll be glad to hear from researchers at America's Northwestern University that less than 10% of children have daily temper tantrums; and from our NHS that they are usually outgrown by the age of four.

After – and even before – this age, frequent, violent and unpredictable tantrums may indicate a psychological problem, and if you are concerned about your child's continuing temper, do contact your health visitor or GP. I won't say don't worry, because of course you will, but there are several different and effective therapies available on the NHS; some likely with long waiting lists, but at least you'll have got the ball rolling, and an after-all-not-needed appointment can always be cancelled.

Meanwhile, the Family Lives website gives sound advice about tantrums as well as a free help line for parents on 0808 800 2222. And all I can add to that is my own optimism for, however troubled, every loved and stood-by child.

PICKY EATERS

Who doesn't know one? Who hasn't been one? How come? And what can be done to help?

Let's start by disposing of a common but mistaken, stereotype. Not all picky eaters are poorly nourished or underweight. Much of today's childhood obesity is due to an exclusive preference for high sugar, high fat food.

In both cases how much or how little gets eaten is less important than the lack of variety for a healthy diet. For this, something from the four main food groups (carbohydrate, vegetable-fruit, dairy and protein-meat) should be provided every day.

As for how come, there are some health conditions that account for eating disorders, for example anaemia, reflux and swallowing difficulty which all need medical treatment and advice. There is also evidence of picky eating in different generations of the same family, possibly due to some inherited tendency, though more likely to the parents' own example.

Actually, with healthy children, eating problems rarely occur before the age of two. After, or even while, being weaned, most become accustomed to store-bought or home-blended vegetables, fruit and meat. Then the introduction to different tastes and textures of 'real' food is quite a step-change from months of all that bland and beige, spoon-fed mush.

As this usually happens around the age of two, it is not easy to distinguish wary reluctance from the rebelliousness associated with this stage.

Among my relations, the first reaction of three children (all boys) was to accept only 1) mashed potato, 2) Weetabix cereal, 3) tomato soup with cheese on toast. Perhaps the parents of these three foresaw what is now well known: that pressure is likely to increase a child's aversion to food. In any case, 40 years on 1) spends his holidays climbing Scotland's Monroe mountains, 2) is a sophisticated diner out and 3) a 9th dan black belt karate instructor: apparently none the worse for their early pickiness.

You may remember from the class a more positive explanation for terrible-two behaviour as a normal, healthy expression of independence and self-control. This fits well with advice from the Infant and Toddler Forum that now it's time for parents to hand over the spoon and put up with spills and mess, while toddlers learn the physical and social skills to self-feed, that include the decision (which they are quite capable of making) when enough is enough. Of course you need to be in sight, or at least ear-shot to be aware of choking or any other distress. And don't worry if your child's idea of enough doesn't match your own; it won't be long before the next meal and the chance for a good catch-up.

So far so good. Your child has learned to use a spoon and you, to recognise and respect some self-control over his or her food. Not yet plain sailing for all though, as research shows one third of our children become picky eaters at this stage. To help you avoid, or bring peace to, meal-time battles, here is some more useful advice.

1. Your health visitor will confirm that young children need 3 meals with 2-3 (not more) healthy snacks each day. As far as possible these should be planned around nap and bed times for maximum appetite, minimum fatigue and with zero munchies in between.

2. Meanwhile, keep an eye on your children's intake of milk, hot chocolate, fruit juice and other soft drinks, all of which have enough calories to reduce their appetite for actual food. You could water-down toddlers' night time bottle, and serve only water with all meals.

3. Arrange meal times so they don't have to be rushed (before shopping, bed, TV or story time); also don't drag them out. Toddlers and next-stage children usually eat what they want and need within twenty minutes then, with or without a clean plate, should be allowed to leave the table.

4. As long as your child is well and has age-appropriate weight and height, part or even the whole of a meal, occasionally skipped won't cause any harm. Best not to offer a different dish, though, or any snack between this and the next meal.

5. That said, of course consult your health visitor or GP about any height, weight or other health concerns you may have.

6. As eating is learned behaviour, this is best learned from parents and older siblings at table without the distraction of TV, I-pads or toys.

One supermarket survey records that one in five mothers makes three separate meals for dinner, to suit all likes and dislikes: extra work for them and no favour to any picky eaters who need the physical and social experience of all sorts of different food.

7. At dinner serve two courses, one savoury and one sweet, but don't make the second depend on or serve as a reward for finishing the first. That glamorises sweets in general, shames the child and loses the opportunity for at

least that amount of nourishment. For the same reason, don't offer sweets to upset children; find other ways to comfort their distress.

8.   Pay attention to children when they are eating, not when they are not.

> It is known that pressure of any kind increases food adversity; after-the-fact praise is fine, but don't coax, bribe or even think of punishing children for not eating.
>
> Gone are the days, thank goodness, when children were obliged to stay at table, often alone; sometimes even returning the next day, to finish what was left on last night's plate. Instead just remove the uneaten food without comment and continue with dessert.

9.   Some parents rely on the taste-one-teaspoon rule for any new or unpopular food; not in itself harmful if applied with a light hand, except where it leaves you if refused.

10.   For heading trouble off at the pass, though, some of these suggestions should help.

11.   Knowing that children often eat more and better away from home, a friend of mine, arranging an away play-date, used to ask the mum to make some usually rejected food that would be eaten for politeness sake, and perhaps even eventually liked.

12.   Offer new or unpopular items as finger food (e.g. raw instead of cooked fruit and veg) which most toddlers and many older children enjoy.

13.   Children's tastes change over time, so previously unpopular food is worth trying again.

14. For all, but especially picky eaters, serve food in small portions with the option to ask for more.

15. Serve at least one well-liked food on the plate so they won't go hungry without the rest.

16. Involve your children in menu planning and shopping. Try the supermarket game of letting them choose any three new foods to take home on condition of at least one bite.

17. Ditto food preparation: making it fun with faces on sandwiches and pizza; sprinkles and other decorations on cakes.

18. Always have healthy food and drink available and ready for snacks, instead of biscuits, sweets and sugary pop.

Fast forward a few years and be prepared for your teenage daughter's decision (less common with boys) to become a vegetarian. What? More picky eating when you thought that was all over and done? Actually this may be her first socially ethical choice which, however inconvenient, deserves your active encouragement. Well worth the cost of a special cook book, your help in the kitchen and appreciation at the dinner table. More than likely this is a phase that won't last very long, but by no means a waste of effort and time. What you'll have done is help develop a social conscience that, over time, will find other causes to support and well justify your pleasure and pride.

Meanwhile there's more information and advice to be found in books by Lucy Cook & Laura Webber (Stressful Feeding) and Jane Ogden (The Good Parenting Food Guide), as well as the website www.bda.uk/food facts

And from me, one last, perhaps the most useful of all previous suggestions: try to make meal time a comfortable experience for the whole family, with general, not food-related conversation. It's things like anyone's latest news and views, welcome visitors, word games, 'what-would-you-do-if' questions, and the example of parents' own relaxed attitude that allow picky eaters, in their own good time, to try and accept enough of the different kinds of food recommended for their growth, general well-being and health.

—RECIPES—

BREAD
(For 1 Loaf or 12 Rolls)

5 cups of white (or half white/half whole grain) flour, 2 cups warm water, 1 tsp sugar, 1 tsp salt, 1 packet dried yeast and 1 tbsp vegetable oil

1. Oil or grease loaf tins or baking sheets.

2. Put sugar and yeast in a cup to soak with ½ cup of the recipe water while measuring the other ingredients.

3. Sieve flour and salt into a large bowl.

4. Add yeast mixture and oil, stirring with a fork.

5. Add remaining, still warm, water and keep stirring till lumps form, then use your hands to shape the dough into a single lump.

6. Lightly sprinkle a table or board with flour and knead (pull, push, roll and thump) the dough till it has a springy, elastic feel (5 – 10 minutes).

7. Place dough in a large oiled bowl, cover with a tea towel and leave in a warm place, at least an hour, to rise.

8. Twice-risen bread is best, if you have the time, in which case remove, punch down and briefly knead the dough, then return to bowl and let rise again as before.

9. Then pat, roll and shape into 1 loaf or 12 equal-size rolls, place in/on tins or trays.

10.   Brush tops with milk or beaten egg, sprinkle with flour or salt or seeds (all optional, fine with none).

11.   Place into cold oven. Turn on to 350 F/180 C, bake, checking rolls after 40 minutes/loaves after 55 minutes.

(By this time, young children may have lost interest, and would have been quite satisfied with the once-risen result, so skip number 8, above, and proceed from number 9).

12.   Have some fresh butter and jam ready, and ignore the old rumour that freshly-baked bread causes indigestion. I can find no evidence of that, and suspect it's been put about by old wives knowing day-old bread is less delicious and won't get eaten up so soon.

CAMPFIRE BREAD
(AKA Dampers)

For 4-6 people you will need: 1 lb/500 g plain or self-raising flour, 1 tsp salt, enough water to make a soft dough, a mixing bowl and spoon and several 'green' sticks (hazel is best) cut from a nearby hedge.

In advance or on site, mix, then wrap a small handful of dough around the end 3 or 4 inches of each stick. Once the fire burns down a bit, 'campers,' including children, hold and turn a stick above the embers (not flames) till their damper is nicely brown, then removed, and the hole filled with butter, jam/honey/Marmite or a previously cooked sausage with ketchup or mustard as preferred.

The fun and open-air appetite will more than make up for any twigs or ashes consumed.

COLD WITCH

(Doesn't qualify as a healthy snack, but it's fun to make, tastes great, and surely won't hurt for an occasional treat.)

1-2 packets 'Nice' (oblong & very plain) biscuits, ½lb /225g coconut fat, ½ lb/225g icing sugar, 2 eggs, 1 cup cocoa powder, 1 tsp coffee granules.

Grease and line loaf tin with cling-film. Gently melt fat in pan and allow to cool a little, whisk in all the rest, pour about ¼ inch into tin, cover with layer of biscuits, repeat several times and finish with top layer of chocolate mix. Chill several hours, then turn out and serve thin slices.

BUTTER

1. Beat 1½ pints/850ml double cream with an electric mixer until it separates into curds and whey. This takes between 5 – 7 minutes; as it thickens, and is quite hard work for the motor which might need a moment's 'mid-stream' rest. A turn-handle beater takes longer, offering the chance for more than one child to take turns.

2. Scoop the curds into a sieve over a bowl before submerging them in very cold water to draw off any remaining whey.

3. With a firm hand, squeeze the curds into a solid mass.

4. At this point you can add, in another bowl, a drop or two of yellow food colouring for a more authentic look, and/or a pinch of salt.

5. Roll it up in greaseproof paper and put to chill in the fridge.

Having no preservatives, it won't last as long as butter, but tasting so good, you won't have to worry about that.

Those who like baking might want to keep the whey, as it's very good in soda bread or scones.

SHAKEN NOT STIRRED

Butter made with marbles in a jar may be more fun for one or any number of kids. The bigger the jar the longer it takes so, depending on age, consider baby-food, regular jam pots and all sizes in between, then all you need are few glass marbles and enough whipping (whipping at least 35%) or double cream to half fill the chosen jar(s).

Drop 2 or 3 marbles into each half-filled jar.

Tightly screw on lid and start shaking, as hard and long as you can till the cream starts to thicken.

There's no harm opening the lid to check from time to time, but don't give up till there are solid curds inside, separated from the whey.

After this, just follow instructions from number 2 above.

Writing this, I've just realised why, as children, we always did this on the grass outside, where dropped jars wouldn't break and spilled cream need no cleaning up.

THREE CHOICES OF JAM

Ingredients

900g/2 lbs fruit (blackberries, strawberries or raspberries), prepared weight.
900g/2 lbs granulated sugar.
1 tsp. of butter (walnut size)

1. Put the fruit into a preserving pan or heavy-based saucepan: -

(for blackberries, add 50m /1¾oz water and 1½ tbsp. lemon juice.
(for strawberries, add 3 tbsp. lemon juice (no water).
(for raspberries, add nothing.

2. Bring to boil then lower to simmering heat:-
(for blackberries, 2 minutes.
(for strawberries, 5 minutes.
(for raspberries, 2 minutes

By then the fruit should be soft.

3. Tip in the sugar, stirring over very low heat until it is dissolved, then bring to a full rolling boil and, without stirring continue cooking : -
for blackberries 10 – 12 minutes . . .
for strawberries 20 – 25 minutes . . .
for raspberries 5 minutes . . .

. . . or in each case until setting point of 221 F/105 C (or drop a teaspoonful on a plate, leave a few minutes to cool then push it with your finger to one side: if it runs back where it was, cook a bit longer, if it stays put, the jam is ready to set).

4. Remove from the heat, skim off scum with a slotted spoon, stir in the butter to dissolve any that remains, leave for 15 minutes while the fruit settles, then pour into sterilised jars.

POTATO CRISPS

Children from the age of six or seven can help with the preparation though, of course, need close attention when near the frying pan.

1. Clean and peel as many potatoes as you need to make the amount of crisps you want.

2. With a knife, vegetable peeler, grater or gadget blade, make the thinnest possible slices (best not more than 1/8 inch thick) and place in a bowl of cold water to prevent discolouration.

3. Pour enough cooking oil for deep frying into a large saucepan and heat to 300 F /149 C.

4. Drain and dry potato slices. (From here on, do not crowd them; cook in several batches with just a single layer in the pan).

5. Submerge slices in the hot oil for a few minutes then, while still white, remove with a slotted spoon to a dish covered with paper towel.

6. Increase the oil heat to 350F/177C, re-submerge slices and cook until they golden and crisp.

7. Remove to fresh paper towel, and pat lightly to remove any excess oil before serving with – if you like – salt and vinegar.

Crisps can also be made from sweet potatoes and other vegetables like carrots, parsnips, beetroot and courgettes. Recipes for these can be found online by Googling homemade vegetable crisps.

Double frying won't be necessary if, after stage 3, you boil the drained slices for 3 minutes in 2 quarts of water with 2 tbsp. vinegar; dry them on paper towels and continue from stage 4.

PEANUT BUTTER

Ingredients: any quantity of salted or plain peanuts, salt and sugar to taste.

The most fun for children making this is with an old-fashioned kitchen table mincer through which the nuts are put three times.

The first time just a lot of crumbs come out; the second time lots of lumpy little 'worms'; and the third time a nice smooth paste that may be seasoned with a little sugar and/or salt. Occasionally, depending on brand or age of peanuts, a fourth put-through may be needed

OR, because not everyone can lay hands on those old mincers: -

The peanuts can be blitzed in a food processor with a series of short bursts to avoid over heating the motor, because it takes quite a while. Don't give up, though; just push crumbs down from the side with a spatula, and keep going till you have the texture (chunky or smooth) of your choice, which you may want to season as above.

STOVE TOP POP CORN

1. With cooking ring on medium setting, heat 1 tsp vegetable oil in a large lidded saucepan.

2. From 1/3 cup of un-popped corn, add 3 or 4 kernels and cover with lid.

3. When they start popping add remaining corn in an even layer; replace lid, remove pan from heat and count 30 seconds (Counting out loud together is fun for the kids).

4. Return pan to the heat, and the corn will soon start popping. Once in full swing, shake pan over the heat, with the lid slightly ajar to let out the steam and keep the popcorn crisp.

5. When pops slow down to 4 or 5 seconds apart, remove pan from heat and tip contents into a wide bowl; keep warm while melting butter (perhaps with syrup, Marmite, soy, or chili sauce) to drizzle over corn when served. Grated cheese on top is a popular choice in my family.

With this method, nearly all kernels pop and none gets burnt.

MICROWAVE POPCORN 1

A cup of un-popped corn, vegetable oil, salt to taste.

1. In a small bowl stir oil into corn.

2. Tip into a brown paper lunch bag, sprinkle with salt (if wanted) and double-fold down top of bag.

3. Cook on full power for $2\frac{1}{2}$ – 3 minutes till pops come 2 – 3 seconds apart.

4. Carefully open bag to avoid steam, pour into a wide bowl, and proceed from number 6 on previous page.

MICROWAVE POPCORN 2

A quarter cup un-popped corn, 2 tbsp butter, salt to taste.

1. Place kernels in $2\frac{1}{2}$ quart lidded microwave bowl.

2. Close lid and cook on high till pops come 3 seconds apart (likely about 4 minutes).

3. Remove from oven, pour into a wide bowl, and proceed from number 6 on previous page.

MAYONNAISE

The easiest way to make this is with a stick blender and fitted cup, for which you need: -

1 egg yolk
2 tbsps. water
1 tbsp. lemon juice
1 tsp Dijon mustard
1 cup olive or vegetable oil
salt to taste.

Place egg yolk, water, lemon juice and mustard in the cup.

Pour oil on top and allow to settle for 30 seconds.

Place stick in the cup and switch on.

As the mixture begins to thicken, gently tilt and lift the stick until all oil is absorbed.

Add salt if needed, and store in sealed containers for up to 2 weeks in the fridge.

Over and done in no time and perhaps with less chance to involve children than when made, with the following recipe, using a hand-turned or electric whisk.

2 eggs yolks
1 tsp Dijon mustard
18 oz/500ml mixed vegetable oil
1-2 tbsp. white wine vinegar
juice of ½ a lemon
salt to taste.

Whisk egg yolks in a bowl, first without, then with the mustard.

Gradually and very slowly add half the oil, whisking continuously for about 5 minutes until thickened.

Whisk in 1 tbsp. vinegar to loosen the mixture.

Gradually, still whisking, add the remaining oil.

Season with salt, a squeeze of lemon juice and more vinegar if needed.

Store as above in the fridge.

The discarded egg whites can be frozen and used another time to make, also child-popular, meringues.

TOMATO KETCHUP

Slow cooker version:

2 1lb/500gr tins of puréed tomatoes
¼ cup water (divided)
¼ cup white sugar
½ cup white wine vinegar
½ tsp onion powder,
¼ tsp garlic powder
a pinch each of mustard powder, black pepper and celery salt
1 whole clove

1. Put tomato purée in the slow cooker; swirl 2 oz. water round each empty can and add that too.

2. Add all other ingredients and stir well.

3. Cook on high, uncovered, until reduced by half and very thick (10 – 12 hours), stirring every hour or so.

4. Remove the clove (if you can find it), pour into bottles or jars and store, up to 3 weeks in the fridge.

UNCOOKED VERSION

1 6oz /170g tin of tomato paste
½ cup white wine or apple cider vinegar
1 tsp each mustard powder and sugar or honey (not both)
½ tsp each powdered cumin, any preferred dried herb and table salt.

Combine all ingredients in a bowl and mix well. For a less vinegary taste, substitute water for some of that vinegar.

PIZZA DOUGH

Popular with children are pizza parties where each has a base to cover with sauce and their choice from a selection of prepared toppings, including cheese which older children can grate for themselves.

Supermarkets sell ready-made bases, but if you prefer to make them yourself, here is a tried and true recipe for 1 large or 3 small ones which you can double or triple according to need.

9 oz/260 grams plain white flour, $\frac{3}{4}$ tsp each of sugar and dried yeast
5 fluid oz./140 ml warm water, 1 tsp salt & 2tbsp vegetable oil

1. Mix all together in a large bowl, then knead 5 minutes as for bread.

2. Cover with a damp cloth and leave $1\frac{1}{2}$ hours to rise.

3. Have ready enough oiled and lightly floured baking trays, and preheat oven 400 F/ 200 C.
Pat and stretch dough into required number of bases & prick each 5 or 6 times with a fork.

4. Brush lightly all over with oil to avoid a soggy crust.

5. The children can take it from there, spreading tomato sauce (fine from a jar) and chosen fillings.

6. After 'resting' for 10 minutes, the pizzas are ready for 25 minutes in the oven, or they could be frozen for use at another time.

PLAY DOUGH
(Definitely Not For Eating, But Still Fun To Make)

Play dough can be rolled flat, coiled, shaped and cut like regular pastry; it can be used more than once, or shaped, baked and painted for a keep-sake which could be hung on a ribbon through a hole made with a skewer or straw, before it goes into the oven at 300F/145 C for 1 hour.

Recipe 1
Ingredients

1 cup any kind of flour
¼ cup of salt
½ cup warm water
3-5 drops food colouring (optional)

1. Mix together flour and water in a bowl, water and food colouring in a jug or cup.

2. Slowly pour water onto the flour, stirring till it all holds together.

3. Knead with your hands to distribute the colouring, rolling in a little more flour if too sticky for modelling use.

Recipe 2

This version is made the same way with added ingredients for more elasticity. Once made, both should be covered and stored until needed in the fridge.

Ingredients

2 cups any kind of flour
2 cups warm water
1 cup salt
2 tbsp. vegetable oil
1 tbsp. cream of tartar
2-3 drops food colouring (optional)

Add oil to the water mix, cream of tartar to the flour, and follow instructions 1 – 3 above.

WARNING: play dough is not good for animals to eat, so beware of any getting dropped or offered to your pets.

SEX EDUCATION

In the 19th century, before sex education was even heard of, poor families with more children than beds at least had the chance to learn from each other, while for the better off there were prostitutes for the boys and for girls facing the 'ordeal' of marital sex, there was often only the mothers' fabled advice to 'lie back and think of England'.

What progress, then, in the 20th century? In spite of the suffragettes, women at work, Marie Stopes contraceptive clinics, and the 1940's post-war baby boom, not much, if my experience is anything to go by.

Sex education in 1958 at one of England's most respected boarding schools was given by the elderly, unmarried head mistress for the protection of all us leavers against the perils of forthcoming bed-sit land. It went something like this: 'In case of day-time visitors (meaning men of course) be sure to have cushion covers on your bed pillows, and don't let them in after dark. Just shake hands on the door step, and if there's any importunity, give them a little push, like this (demonstrating on girl from the front row) and say 'half past ten's my dead-line, young man'!

To be fair about this much-mocked lesson, I must give you the 1963 published advice of agony aunt Katherine Whitehorn: 'The chief trouble, for man or girl, is that everything in a bedsitter is so VISIBLE. Unless you work it all out with greatest care, your visitor can see at a glance just exactly what you expect or hope for or hope to avoid.'

For my best friend at Cheltenham Ladies College (then **the** most respected school), from the house-mistress, it was shorter and, in both senses of the word, more sweet: 'Sex is the icing on the cake, and too much icing will make you sick'!

Luckily we both had brothers, day-school girl friends, pets, farm animals and women's magazines for more useful lessons about the 'facts of life'. Even so sex, for us in those days, was mostly the subject of gossip, secrets, sniggers and smutty jokes, with much still to be learned from better or worse experience.

That's not what I wanted for my own child; I wanted him to be at ease with his body and to know from a young age where and how it came to be. You already know about one of my early attempts at sex education. And here's another one: young Peter seemed not to notice a photo of Michelangelo's naked David on the kitchen wall until the day he brought a friend home from school, and an interesting conversation followed their marker-penned addition, while I was upstairs, of a moustache and Superman underpants. Years later, there were more interesting conversations with my 'other', older children about the different social significance of Picasso's simple line drawing of a naked woman and the page three models of the tabloid press.

Since then there has been an alarming, nationwide, increase of broken marriages, children in care, teenage pregnancies, and sexually transmitted disease. The resulting cost to health and social services may be the reason that, in 1993, sex education was included in the curriculum of all state-maintained secondary schools, and in 2017, in all primary schools as well.

Not everyone was/is happy with this; some finding it a nanny-state step too far, and/or in conflict with their religion. For them, since February 2016, the government has allowed their children to be opted out.

Of those in favour, I expect many are glad to be absolved from the embarrassment of their own explanations, though some, I do know, have found the school lessons opened the door to long-delayed discussions at home.

On whichever side of the fence you find yourselves you should be aware that, intended or not, children's sex education begins long before that, at home.

The way their bodies are handled (range duty-pleasure), parents' attitude (uptight- relaxed) to bodily functions; any different treatment of boys and girls, even parents own (distant-close) relationship: it's from things like this that children draw conclusions about their own sexuality.

The Sex Education Forum (www.ncb.org.uk/sef) and a recent NHS campaign ('Sex Worth Talking About') each recommend teaching children about sex from a very young age, and both offer answers to common questions that will help you off to a good start.

1. How young?

As soon as they ask questions about sex, they are ready for – not stork or cabbage patch tales - just brief, but truthful answers. If, out of embarrassment, you keep putting this off, you'll find the longer you wait, the harder it will be. Meanwhile, the child you've been happily washing and changing since birth will be more comfortable with simple explanations now than later when these things are done in private and alone.

2. How much should they be told?

No more than they have asked, for example: 'Where do babies come from?' doesn't need the whole story from conception; 'Babies grow in mummy's tummy until they're big enough and ready to come out', might well be enough. To a follow-up question then or later: 'How does the baby get in there?' you could answer 'From a seed that daddy puts in', and to 'How does it get out?' 'Through mummy's special passage that's the vagina'.

> I know some parents prefer nick-names for body parts, and there's nothing wrong with that, but children should also know the text-book terms that will be used in lessons at school.

And you could follow up daddy's seed planting with a generally reliable bean in a pot to be fed, watered and watched while it grows.

You could also take advantage of upcoming/expected births (babies, puppies, kittens, etc.) to introduce the subject yourselves.

> Curious Peter's discovery of Tampax in our bathroom seemed a good opportunity to explain about women's menstruation that needed a sort of inside bandage to manage the blood. Without the slightest embarrassment, just drawing on his own experience of blood and bandages, his only, and kind, concern was whether my periods hurt, which I thought pretty nice from a 5-year old.

3. What else do children need to know about sex?

The time will come for their knowledge of body changes at puberty, of contraception, sexually transmitted diseases and same-sex relationships. These subjects are all on the curriculum and will be covered in age-appropriate stages at school. Meanwhile, for pre-schoolers at home, what they most need to know is that it's OK and easy to talk about sex with at least one of their parents.

> I know a family where a close and trusted relative was a 'good enough' substitute for both 'uneasy' parents.

The explicitness of school sex education is often countered by parents' personal discretion that leaves children to speculate about, literally, 'the shape of things to come'.

One way to satisfy their curiosity without sniggers is, from an early age, to have art books or even pictures of naked adults (male and female) about the house, or National Geographic magazine which features countries (mostly hot ones) where nakedness is the norm.

> A frame with glass would protect any valued pictures from such permanent indignity as was suffered by the unframed David on my kitchen wall.

4. How does an only child learn about the body difference of the opposite sex?

From a very young age most children see their parents getting dressed and undressed or in the bath and shower. Of course this does no harm and may well suggest some similar difference between boys and girls. This may be tested and proved, if permitted, in naked play with a visiting friend(s) in the garden, on the beach, or more privately, in the bath. Though parents should keep an eye or at least an ear on any 'show-and-tell', this is perfectly natural curiosity, and between children of similar age, no cause for alarm.

> I'm remembering four year-old Peter finding, among a friend's handed-on toys, an open-mouthed doll with a bottle for feeding and a small exit hole on the side of its bum, and his question after long examination: 'Is this meant to be a boy or a girl?' It took almost a year and quite a dent in my

budget to track down a pair of realistic (girl and boy) dolls. Unfortunately, by the time they arrived, that ship had sailed and they stayed untouched in their box until found a new home. For your information, though, several internet sites are now advertising 'anatomically correct', multi-cultural and much more affordable boy and girl dolls.

5. Sex education before puberty: is it either necessary or worth spoiling childhood innocence?

It's things like harshness, prudery, ignorance and insensitivity that can spoil a child's innocence, not those that have been suggested here. As for puberty: the average age, which for our parents – and theirs – was thirteen, is now often reached as young as nine. That is one of many good reasons for sex education in primary schools, which all parents are advised to contact and learn more about.

6. All right then, for primary school, but that's enough; in secondary kids need to be getting their heads down and passing exams.

I don't think you would say that if you'd overheard, in a recent year-ten sex education class, the teacher reading out these anonymous questions: -

'Can you get pregnant by just kissing?'

'Should you believe girls when they say they're on the pill?'

'You don't actually get pregnant on the first time, do you?'

'Is it true you can't get pregnant from sex done standing up?'

By the time young people are dating, parents' attempts to discourage unsuitable relationships are well known to have the opposite effect. That's one of the good reasons we now have (since 2013) sex <u>and</u> relationship education in UK secondary schools.

7. What should you do when your child hasn't shown any interest in sex before entrance to secondary school?

Well, he or she has probably learned quite a lot already, from primary school classes and peers. But you could leave a next-stage instruction book somewhere likely to be found which might lead to some actual conversation, and anyway, at least provide the chance of some useful catching up.

Years ago, my cousins were worried their nine year-old son was uninterested in story books and behind in reading at school. One weekend, when the family was camping in our field, I put a humorously illustrated book (Where did I come from? by Peter Mayle and Arthur Robins) in his tent, which remained firmly zipped up for the rest of that day. My plan was just to get him reading, but of course the actual subject won't have come amiss. For your information, that book is still available, if not in your local shops, then on the internet.

Other good books on the subject include, for 4 years plus: -

<u>Mummy Laid an Egg by Babette Cole</u>

<u>Where Willy Went by Nicholas Allan</u>

<u>Facts of Life Growing Up</u> (Susan Meredith & Robyn Gee), for adolescents, and for parents there's lots of useful online advice from 'Facts of Life' (www.fpa.org.uk) and

from the Speakeasy Sex Education Course (with David Kesterton at Cornwall's 'Healthy Schools') which provides a phone number for individual help and advice.

Now just one last word from me: the best foundation for any child's sex and relationship education is the parents own open, relaxed, confident attitude to the subject AND to each other.

BED WETTING

"Parents' recently improved attitude to, and treatment of, bed wetting owes less to psychological enlightenment than to the invention of the automatic washing machine."

This light-hearted, possibly exaggerated, claim made perfect sense to me when I heard it in a psychology class more than forty years ago. Throughout my childhood I never even saw a washing machine, but I did know a boarding-school boy who was made to appear at breakfast with the last night's wet pyjamas tied round his neck. This practice was not uncommon at the time, so thank goodness for whatever part washing machines played in our psychological enlightenment.

Of course today's parents would be horrified at that kind of cruelty, but many are still uncertain of the best way to help their bed-wetting child, so for them, here is some useful information and advice.

Bed wetting is common for children up to the age of five or six, though some three year-olds are mostly dry at night, and some of eleven or twelve still are not. 'Night-time continence' often comes later for boys than it does for girls.

As bed wetting is never deliberate, and rarely even conscious, any reproof or punishment is not only unfair, but also likely to make matters worse. Why? Because this is one of many childhood problems known to be triggered by worry and stress.

My own, and many others', experience of this is a recurrent dream about midnight's perilous path from the bedroom, the safe arrival in the toilet, the relief of getting there in time, and then the dreadful betrayal of waking up to the last warm trickle onto already sodden sheets.

1. Bed wetting is also one of those childhood problems for which prevention is better than cure, and the following advice from the NHS will help any uncertain parents off to a good start.

2. Make sure your child has plenty to drink during the day: 6-8 glasses of, preferably not fizzy, water: none in the last hour before bed, though for the still thirsty child, just a few drops won't hurt.

3. Cut down, or even cut out caffeine-based drinks which over stimulate the bladder: that means all colas, coffee, tea and, sorry, many children's favourite chocolate milk.

4. The need of most healthy children to pee four to seven times a day gives parents that many chances to encourage and reward their use of the toilet. This will help the bladder awareness needed at night.

5. Avoid carrying your sleeping or woken child to the toilet. Although that may be a good short-term solution, it is also one that delays his/her own response to signals from the bladder. Better to rely a bit longer on the night nappy instead.

6. With the back-up of a water proof mattress cover, a low-lit landing or space between bed and bathroom may be the path to success. In case of accidents, though, have fresh sheets nearby for changing with the minimum of fuss.

7. Soak wet bedding in a mild solution of cold water and bleach before washing in the usual way.

8. There are medicines that can increase bladder capacity or reduce the amount of urine produced by the kidneys. These may be prescribed by your GP for a few week's trial, the occasional sleep-over, or nights away at camp.

9. If none of these measures work, you could try a bed-wetting alarm. This is a small sensor attached to night-wear that wakes the child as soon as it gets wet, eventually triggering the same response for his/her own signals. It is not provided by the NHS, but can be bought from a charity known as ERIC (Education and Resources for Improving Childhood Incontinence), www.eric.org.uk .

ERIC's very similar advice also includes the possibility of physical causes for bed wetting such as: an unusually small bladder, over-active kidneys or just sleep too deep to notice any warning signals. A related physical cause could be the knock-on effect of constipation with a swollen bowel putting undue pressure on the bladder. Or, as persistent bed wetting often runs in families, it could be inherited from either parent, or even both.

None of these conditions is common or immediately apparent, but if you do find reason to suspect a health problem, please contact your health visitor or GP. Meanwhile here, from my own experience, is some more practical advice.

Most important of all the Don'ts is not to blame or punish your bed-wetting child of no matter what age. Everything else can, and will here, be expressed as Do's.

1. Once your child is potty trained, you can try bed time without nappies as long as you don't expect instant success. Occasional lapses are almost inevitable at this stage.

2. Actually it often helps switching from nappies to those padded pull-up pants at least a few nights before doing without either protection.

3. First thing in the morning, wet or dry, take your child to the toilet to establish that good habit.

4. After a dry night, praise or reward your child for all his/her good 'grown-up' preventions: things like the type, timing and number of drinks and remembering, asking or agreeing to use the toilet during the day. Tempting as it may be, celebration of the actual dry bed risks his/her sense of failure when it is not.

5. Despite your best efforts older children are likely to learn from friends or class-mates to be ashamed of still wetting the bed. To save them further embarrassment at home it often helps to demonstrate the use of washer and dryer so they can strip and remake their own bed without any, unless wanted, comment or advice.

You will be interested to know that five is the average age for night-time continence. 'Average' is the important word here because children are all different and bladders pay no heed to calendars, nor work to any predetermined rule.

So, after all, just one more Don't: don't compare your child's progress with those of friends in case your – or their – earlier success undermines the relaxed parental confidence that allows children to reach the dry-night goal in their own good time.

ADHD
(Attention Deficit and Hyperactivity Disorder)

Twenty years ago most people, including me, had never heard of this, although it had been identified and labelled long before then. Nowadays almost every person has come across those initials and knows, if little else, at least that they spell trouble.

My first experience of the 'disorder' was in September 1994 with the referral of a six year-old boy recently expelled, for unmanageable behaviour, from primary school. Actually his label was just ADD (Attention Deficit Disorder) which I, knowing no better, mistook for lack of parental attention.

Of course there have been troublesome children throughout history; their problems studied, recorded and 'explained' as long ago as the 18th century. It was not until the 1930s, though, that a syndrome of annoying, exhausting and self-defeating behaviour was identified and attributed to a lack of focus (attention deficit), and constant restlessness (hyperactivity) that was, and still is, three times more common in boys than girls.

Since then much of the research into causes and treatment has taken place in the United States which may account for my early ignorance as well as the ADD label given to that little boy who was born, raised and only just returned from America.

Not all researchers have agreed about the influence of nature or nurture (heredity or environment) on this condition which may occur in different generations of the same family and, for a third of those affected will not be outgrown; begging the question whether genes or parents' example is to 'blame'.

Not all doctors and social scientists have agreed about the available treatments: medication and social support, either or both at the same time or spaced apart; and from confirmed sceptics, no medication; just a good parenting class.

Recently a third symptom: 'impulsivity' has been added to the inattentiveness (attention deficit) and extreme activity (hyperactivity) of the syndrome for each of which here is a list of typical signs.

The inattentive child:

• Has trouble staying focussed on tasks or play

• Makes careless mistakes

• Doesn't pay attention to detail

• Appears not to listen when spoken to

• Has difficulty remembering things and following instructions

• Gets bored with projects and tasks before they are completed

• Frequently loses or misplaces homework, books, toys etc.

• Has trouble staying organised and planning ahead

The hyperactive child:

• Constantly fidgets and squirms

• Often leaves seat when sitting quietly is expected or required

• Talks excessively

• Has difficulty playing quietly or relaxing

• Moves around, runs and climbs at inappropriate times and places

• May have a quick temper or 'short fuse'

• Is always 'on the go'

The impulsive child:

• Acts without thinking rather than takes time

• Blurts out answers in class without waiting to hear the whole question

• Can't wait for his/her turn in games

• Says the wrong thing at the wrong time

• Often interrupts others

• Intrudes on others people's conversations or games

• Guesses rather than takes time to solve problems

• Has little control over powerful emotions that may result in tantrums or rage

• Has poor social skills

I expect some of you are thinking 'surely most of that's just normal kid behaviour', which might well be true up to the age of four or five. By then most children have learned to pay attention to others, to sit quietly when told, and not to blurt out every brief feeling or thought.

These signs of ADHD are usually evident by the age of seven, though the listed symptoms may not occur to the same extent in every child. Some, with fewer or none of any one symptom group may still be diagnosed with that condition. As epilepsy, thyroid, hearing and some psychological disorders have similar symptoms, of course these must first be considered and ruled in or out.

In any case a doctor is needed to confirm an ADHD diagnosis and prescribe treatment that may, or not, include methylphenidate, more commonly known now as Ritalin. In the 1990s this, although an actual stimulant, was found to have a calming effect on hyperactive children and soon became the quick fix for the condition in the United States, and not long after also in Britain.

What happened next was an extraordinary surge, on both sides of the Atlantic, in the number of children diagnosed with ADHD: in Britain between 2007 and 2012 the recorded increase was 50% and found by the NHS to affect between $2\frac{1}{2}$ – 4% of the population. More dramatic is America's record, between 1991 and 1999, of a 500% increase, affecting, in different states, from 11 to 18.7% of the population.

Of course, statistics like these raise(d) a whole lot of questions: what's going on? Is this some sort of epidemic? Are more just badly behaved children being misdiagnosed, or is it the long-delayed 'promise' of effective medical treatment bringing so many genuine case to light?

> Throughout my child and adulthood I knew only two children with asthma; then in the 1990s I worked in a residential unit where five of the nine children were regular users of Ventolin. My knowledge and experience of allergies was much the same: few and far between fifty years ago; now the high profile subject of public health warnings and regulations for all providers of food. Does this mean those are psychological or scape-goat conditions exploited by pharmaceutical companies, or genuine physical ailments just waiting in the wings, like ADHD, for effective medical treatment?

While medical and social scientists disagree about the causes, treatment and even the existence of the condition, it seems that answers to those questions depend more on opinion than actual facts.

There is common ground, however, for a growing concern about the possible side-effects of Ritalin. Those recorded include sleep problems (insomnia), mood swings, headaches, nausea, loss of appetite, obesity and the inhibition of growth (height and/or weight).

No doubt this accounts for the second thoughts of professional organisations like Britain's National Institute of Health Care Excellence (NICE) and America's Academy of Paediatrics (AAP) as well as medical and social scientists around the world. There is now widespread agreement that Ritalin should be used as a last (not first) resort, only after or combined with other therapies (psychological, physical or occupational) alongside social and community support for children and parents as well.

*   *   *   *   *

Perhaps you have read this far out of concern for a particular, possibly your own, child. I have worked with enough ADHD children to know how troublesome and exhausting they can be, and how tempting may be the quick-fix of prescribed medication. Please, though, do first take advantage of the social, physical and educational support in your community which you can find out about from the Attention Deficit Disorder and Support Service (ADDISS), phone number 020 8952 2800.

Meanwhile here's something you should know and remember in times of trouble: ADHD does not cause bad behaviour; it is our response to it that does that.

I'm thinking of a recent TV documentary about a nine or ten year-old boy with cerebral palsy wreaking havoc at home and school: yelling, swearing, kicking furniture and any person nearby. The response of supervising adults (helpless) and the programme presenter (sympathetic) implied that his condition was the cause. Mine would have been to ask what's the payoff for such behaviour, and where or who did he learn it from?

While it is right to expect and make allowances for the difficulties of all 'handicapped' children, it is a big mistake to let them get away with unacceptable behaviour.

Of course cerebral palsy is a different condition, but I believe it's a fair comparison, and what you already know about the incentives and consequences of behaviour management applies just as well (only more and more often) to children with ADHD.

Finally, here are some comforting positives for you to keep in mind: -

ADHD has nothing to do with intelligence or talent; many such children can be wonderfully imaginative and creative.

With their brain buzzing several ideas at once, they can become master problem-solvers, seeing solutions that other people miss.

When motivated they will work and play hard and strive to succeed in tasks and projects that interest them.

Though exasperating at times, they are never boring; even and often good company and fun.

These are all things you can encourage, enjoy and be proud of in your ADHD child.

Signs and symptoms of ADHD are often present in children with Asperger's or high-functioning Autism, for whom medical and social support is also advisable and, nowadays, widely available.

SIBLINGS

Have you ever wondered why some children brought up by the same parents can turn out to be so different, and whether to expect the same for your own?

While the nature-nurture debate swings back and forth as to the influence of heredity and environment on child development, there can be little doubt about the part played by genes when it comes to physical appearance. Older relatives and photo albums often confirm similar stature, features and colouring passed on from one generation to the next. With very few medical exceptions, there is nothing that can, or need, be done about that.

As for the inheritance of personality, traits like aggression, timidity, impatience, moodiness or self-control, social scientists can only claim tendencies which will themselves be influenced by the child's environment. And that, for the first, second and any following children will be far from the same.

Just think about the experience of a typical first and newly equipped baby; proudly shown off, showered with presents from admiring relatives and friends, marvelled for every burp, smile and tottering step, hovered over day and night by anxious parents swayed this way and that between professional and friendly advice; constantly cooed at, cuddled and photographed: a little prince/princess with the king and queen all to him or herself.

Then compare this, for better and for worse, with the very different world of a second child. Aside from any changes in family circumstances, s/he has, although the same, still quite different parents: with more experience, and confidence, but much less time for photos and doting round the clock.

This child won't know or care about hand-me-down clothes and toys, will think nothing of sharing a room and the parents' attention with a sibling likely to be, at times, a role-model, protector, tormentor or friend. Of course the second child is going to have a different character from the first, and any still to come, as each one finds space and place for a role as leader, follower, know-all, peace-maker, organiser or family clown. Observant parents won't need any professional to explain the influence of environment on their children's personality.

While there may be some genetic influence on those chosen roles, the gains and losses of all siblings are experienced in, and largely due to, their environment. Unlike heredity, this is something over which parents can, and should, right from the start, have some control, starting perhaps with timing of the second and any following births.

Actually there is no golden rule for age spacing children, just some well-known positives and negatives to earlier and later options.

Sooner the better for shared company, passed-on clothes, equipment and toys; child care over and done with in time for parents' other ambitions and pursuits. Sooner the worse for noisy, disorderly days, unrestful nights, and less chance for individual attention to each child, never mind grown-up time to share.

All these considerations may be over-ridden by others more practical and pressing to do with health, finances, employment prospects or simply not enough space in your present house. Whatever your decision it won't alter the fact that, for better or worse, siblings are related longer than any other member of the nuclear family, and here are some tried and true ways to avoid the most common sibling problems, and help you all enjoy each other's company.

1. If your child is old enough to be told there is another baby on the way, the chance to feel, talk to and suggest names for the bump is bound to spark interest; hopefully also good will. It is also wise to warn that babies cry, puke and sleep a lot before they get to be much fun.

2. Let your child, girl or boy, practice holding, feeding and bathing a doll.

3. Unless this is to be a home delivery, explain the child-care arranged for your absence: best with dad or a well-known friend so the new baby won't be associated with strangeness and grief.

4. Encourage visiting friends to match their Oohs and Aahs for the baby with focus on the older child(ren), and, in case any come without 'jealousy presents', have a ready supply of your own.

5. Praise any of your first child's patience, forbearance or help with the baby; also give a sympathetic ear, even compensation, for any justified grumps and gripes.

6. Extra dad-time will be doubly appreciated: by the child for his company and by mum for one-to-one time with the baby, or even just the chance to sleep.

7. Arrange some baby-free times for your child with a popular relative or friend.

8. To give yourselves some time-out while the baby sleeps, try using the kitchen timer for a realistic period of your first child's own quiet play. This often works better if s/he is allowed to set the timer, and gets praise or a small reward for even brief cooperation. This is also very useful for impartial and unchallengeable timing of children taking turns.

Simple jigsaw puzzles can be quietly absorbing, and those of Britain/the World, with each piece a whole county/country, can be useful to, and managed by, even young children with previous assisted practice.

9. Try not to let baby-care interfere with your first child's bed time routine. The day's review, the unravelling of problems and worries, the comfort of favourite stories, the tucking up and final cuddle: these things are not only the best preparation for that night's sleep, but also for the next day's confidence, self-respect and good humour.

Sibling rivalry is normal, natural and not necessarily vicious though, mismanaged, it can be the cause of lasting enmity and grief.

The rivals' goal is usually to get the bigger share of your attention (either by honest effort or by knobbling the opposition, which may be avoided in the case of an equal reward for a jointly-set task).

Where there are more than two children the challenge for parents is to find, for each new-comer, some version of suggestions 1-9 without short-changing the rest. So here are a few more tactics for your consideration.

10. For those old enough to understand make sure they know what is and is not acceptable behaviour.

11. Tired as you may be, one or other parent try for even a few moments of one-to-one time with each child every day.

12. Encourage the older ones to help or keep an eye on the rest, but not so long or so often as to cause resentment of those in their charge.

13. All children need their own space: if possible in their own bedroom; if not, in a shared room arranged with separate 'sacred' areas and furniture for each one's treasures and toys.

14. All children have their good and not so good qualities, to be rewarded or 'worked on'. Comparisons intended to encourage good behaviour are best avoided as the smugness of the one and the resentment of the other will most likely be the only result.

15. When you identify a particular trouble-maker, a private telling-off avoids any gloating and pious provocation from the rest.

16. Where you find equal blame an equal and shared punishment, like NO TV or early bed for all is quite appropriate.

17. Try letting wrong-doers suggest their own punishment: you may be surprised how much worse theirs, than yours, would have been.

18. For older children at odds encourage their own conflict resolution by talking things over, while you stand by, when needed as referee.

19. An occasional or regular gripe session can be useful for airing complaints about siblings, house-rules, also even parents themselves. Sometimes it can be a real eye-opener; often a problem-solver, calmer-down or cheerer-up; but not without your, believe me, life-long example of genuine attention and respect.

Over the years I have come across some families with siblings still nursing old grievances, still competing like children, and others permanently estranged, not knowing or caring where each other lives. What a sad disappointment for their parents. How come? I can only guess: for them something to do with their upbringing, but can now expect you and yours to be opening presents, pulling crackers, stuffing on turkey and trimmings, all together at Christmas for years to come.

P.S. 'Imaginary friends' come in all shapes and sizes: (e.g. older or younger sibling, grandparent, super-hero, princess, protective dragon, amenable pet). The fact that so many children (around 60%) have one, shows it to be quite normal and not a worrying, pathetic consolation for the real thing. Far from it: research, from the University of Melbourne, shows that these children are more articulate, creative, 'socially advantaged' and, actually, better at getting on with their class-mates. So, by all means lay an extra place at table for your child's 'friend', but leave it at that. This is a precious and private relationship, not to be challenged, questioned, mentioned or shared with anyone else, (including you), or it is likely to disappear and be sadly missed.

P.P.S. That said, any such 'friendships' after the age of six may indicate real relationship problems which need professional help.

SPECIAL NEEDS

How many expectant parents have you heard saying they'd be equally happy with a boy or a girl 'as long as it has the right number of fingers and toes'? That's usually a kind of code for other things they'd rather not think of, never mind discuss. Perhaps you've said the same thing and then found yourself nervously checking hands and feet, while waiting for the doctor's or midwife's 'all clear'.

Thanks to nature, science and good pre-natal care, most babies in 'developed' countries are born healthy, fit and well (98% UK and - possibly with different criteria - 97% USA), but what about the 2% or 3% who are not?

According to WebMD, Partners in Health, 'many birth defects are mild and can be easily treated, [but] some are more serious and can have long term effects, while others, including moderate brain damage, may not be detected for months or even years.' So the medical 'all clear' is no guarantee against such conditions as cerebral palsy, autism, dyslexia or ADHD. Also, of course, children of any age can be 'disabled' by some unforeseen illness or accident.

If any of this matches your experience, your most likely reaction would be shock, grief – perhaps even self-blame; all hard to bear without the support of family and friends. Then comes the time to take stock of the situation: it is what it is, and up to you to make the best of that.

Nowadays raising a child with any kind of handicap is easier that it was in the past. There is more general awareness and understanding, better access to, and amenities in, public buildings. There's also more specialised health and social support from the government, agencies and trusts for most children's special needs (*see* contact details in References and Resources section). In many cases there is also the choice of main-stream or 'special' education. For this, your most important consideration is whether your child would thrive or flounder in a 'normal' class; would stagnate or succeed among peers in a special school. Of course it is your knowledge of the child's character and condition and your impression of the local schools that will inform your decision and choice.

Years ago, a former class-mate of mine had a daughter with multiple 'birth defects' affecting her speech (cleft palate), posture (wry neck) and mobility (permanently useless legs). Fortunately there was no brain damage and her mother's determined campaigning eventually secured her place, with wheel-chair access, in a main stream school where she kept up well, went on to university, studied law and is now a practising solicitor.

Another child I knew, with severe behaviour problems attributed to ADHD, needed the smaller classes with specialist teachers for several years before transferring and succeeding in a main stream school. Now, grown up, he is courteous, calm and happily independent with a steady job and comfortable, well-kept home.

Whatever help, support and choice is available in your community, it's still you with the hourly, daily, seemingly endless responsibility for the special needs of your child, and all I can offer, from my own experience, is some relevant and, hopefully useful, advice.

First, take the long view, and from here on make your goal the same as that of all other parents: the resilience and self-control necessary for eventual independence which, more than likely, will be shared and appreciated by your child.

Some year ago, the previously healthy teenage son of my partner (a single parent) was diagnosed with schizophrenia. In between a series of hospital admissions, he continued to live at home while they both came to terms with their inevitable shock, grief, bewilderment and frustration.

Medicine and the passive symptoms of this condition damped down some, but not all, of the boy's charm and humour; some, but not all, of his typical adolescent initiative and 'attitude'; some but not all, of his pre-illness resilience. With enough of his former self intact, he has been able, and more than willing, to move into a nearby 'home' for adults with a variety of special needs. There he has company, some self-control and, under supervision, has been happy for more than eight years.

This kind of supervised accommodation is often recommended by medical and social-care professionals for young adults with special needs so that, 'when the time comes,' they will not be faced, all at once, with the double loss of both parents and home.

Local authorities must – and in many areas voluntary agencies also do – provide support for children with special needs, ranging from supervised or assisted accommodation, and respite day-care, to grants for improved amenities (e.g. ramps, rails, wheel-in showers) in their own home.

Whether or not you need outside help, you do need to know that everything you have learned 'in class' also applies to children with special needs, whose good and not so good behaviour has much the same motivation and meaning and responds to the same kind of encouragement, prevention and cure.

You may already have discovered – or soon will – the truth of this News International headline and subtext (3rd December, 2010):

> PERSONS WITH DISABILITES ARE NOT WITHOUT ABILITIES: IT IS A LAW OF NATURE THAT WHEN A PERSON IS DEPRIVED OF ONE BODY [FUNCTION], LIKE LOSS OF SIGHT OR HEARING, S/HE IS BESTOWED WITH OTHER STRONG FACULTIES.

It is also important for parents of children with special needs to focus on what they can do, rather than what they can't. This means not waiting on them hand and foot; not removing all obstacles in their path, not rushing to pick them up as soon as they fall; not anticipating and meeting their every want and need. It's often a real eye-opener to see what they can do for themselves.

> Many years ago, a six year old boy, badly injured in a gas explosion, attended a play group where I was a new member of the staff. His face was badly burned and the fingers and thumbs of both hands looked like just useless stumps.
>
> At snack time, unable to read his expressions, I was about to open his packet of crisps when warned off by the glance of a more experienced colleague who knew that he could, would and – between stumps and teeth patiently did – manage to do it by himself.

For children with special needs, as for all others, meeting challenges and finding solutions to problems build the character, resilience, self control and respect necessary for any kind of independence.

Here's another example from my teenage years, when eight year old boy and girl twins stayed a few weeks at my parents' 'summer school'. Before birth the boy's umbilical cord had become twisted around his sister's limbs, and she was born with one short, flipper-like arm and one twisted leg which was strengthened and braced so that she could walk. By the time she came to us, it was astonishing how much more she could do than just walk.

That holiday skipping was the younger children's favourite game; running in, over, under and out while we older ones turned the rope. Nothing daunted, this little girl joined the rest with hip-hop clumping steps; sometimes getting safely in and out, sometimes falling, getting right up to join the queue again – and again for another turn.

The only time she couldn't manage alone was at the beach, getting, without the brace, down to the water's edge. Then her brother knew just how much and how little help she needed to splash, dive and swim, as easily as all the other children, in the sea.

P.S. Where a child with special needs has a sibling, each of them may give, receive and learn just as much from their relationship. But please don't overload one for the sake of the other; both need your individual attention, as well as some time apart.

This, and many similar examples support my conviction that challenges, opportunities, freedom and space are as important to the physical and social development of yours, as of any other child.

In spite, however, of what I said about public awareness and understanding, you may already have found that many people are not comfortable, and don't know how to talk or react to others, of any age, with obvious disabilities.

This is also the case in America where a friend of my family gave birth to a baby boy with Apert syndrome (abnormal development of the skull which distorts the shape and features of the face). Now aged five it is clear that he is fortunate to fall into the half of this population whose intelligence remains unaffected, nevertheless, he and his family sometimes experience indiscreet staring or other kinds of insensitive behaviour in public.

So all credit to his mother for her timely intervention with staring by-standers: 'His name is Carl,' she says with a friendly smile, 'you can come and say hello if you like.' Whether or not accepted, surely a brave and worthwhile contribution to public awareness, understanding and tolerance.

Here, applicable on both sides of the Atlantic, is advice from Sheffield's Disability Information Service.

1. Behave naturally and respectfully as you would to any other person.

2. Focus on the person, not on the disability.

3. Talk to the disabled person, not to their assistant or carer.

4. If in doubt whether you are behaving appropriately or using the right language, ask the disabled person.

5. Avoid making assumptions about [his/her] impairment or need.

6. Take care not to make intrusive or personal remarks.

In this way you will be treating a disabled person as you would wish to be.

There is more advice to be found online at Sheffield's Information Service and Wikipedia's Disability Etiquette. These both include today's approved expressions for various aspects of disability. As political correctness is constantly being reviewed and upgraded, some of these may already be out of date, so I'd be less concerned about terminology and more about our attitude and behaviour as listed in 1-6 above.

My own summary of current online advice is not to think of, or describe, anyone in terms of their medical diagnosis (e.g. a paraplegic, an epileptic, a diabetic, a schizophrenic). A person with this or that disability is so much more than any such label and, given the chance, has much to contribute to his/her family, community and even society at large.

Meanwhile, we can all take heart from the following examples of famous people who have overcome known or suspected (the historic ones) childhood disabilities.

Learning difficulties:

Winston Churchill, Albert Einstein, Walt Disney

Epilepsy:
Napoleon, Charles Dickens, marathon runner Alan Blinston

Blindness:
Musicians Stevie Wonder and Ray Charles

Deafness:
Actress Marlee Matlin, world famous percussionist and composer Evelyn Glennie

ADHD:
Film Star Robin Williams

Tourette's Syndrome:
Dan Akroyd

Dyslexia:
Kiera Knightly, Tom Cruise and Sir Richard Branson

Spina Bifida:
Olympic medallist Tanni Grey-Thompson

Stuttering speech:
Bruce Willis, Gareth Gates

Obsessive Compulsive Disorder:
David Beckham, Leonardo DiCaprio

Though famous in their time few, if any, of these names will be known by, or of interest to, the very young, but there are plenty of triumph-over-adversity examples in newspapers, on TV, perhaps even in your own neighbourhood, to encourage and inspire your special needs child. Finally, along with my best wishes, I offer you contact details for agencies which may be of use to you and your family in the References and Resources section of this book beginning on page 206.

BULLYING

> Unwanted aggression from one person [who is] perceived by the other to be more powerful.
>
> —Tom Thelen, Founder of the Victimproof Bullying Prevention Program.

In this brief definition, 'unwanted' and 'perceived' are the most significant words: the first distinguishes bullying from the kind of rough play which many children enjoy, and the second recognises its probable causes and possible cures.

Unfortunately neighbourhood and school-ground bullying are common enough to be taken for granted by some parents, until it happens to their own child.

Then, fathers' instinctive reaction is often to go out and 'teach the bully a lesson', and so it might, but hopefully not just that his child is a cry-baby and tattle-tale, which of course makes matters worse. Neither this nor mothers' impulse to write sick-letters or complaints to school would help the child to face and deal with the problem him or herself.

Generations of bullied children have found little comfort in the old saying about sticks and stones, not much respite in just 'walking away', and not enough courage for the hitting back that risks a fight **and** the adult reproof of another old saying about two wrongs not making a right.

Recent research, however, gives us a better understanding of bullying, and more helpful ways to deal with it.

171

For instance the typical bully, boy or girl, is trying to fulfil so far unmet needs for choice, challenge, self-control and respect. Paradoxically, the typical victim has similar problems causing timidity, uncertainty and vulnerability. These qualities signal an easy mark for bullying that may cause not only anxiety, but also depression, self-harm and, in extreme cases, even suicide.

No parents are going to like the sound of this when all they've done, or are going to do for their children, is the best they can and know how. Of course, please do take credit for that, as you read on for some really effective preventions and cures.

From here on the key word is RESILIENCE. This is defined by Masters et al in a 1950 report to the Joseph Rowntree Foundation as 'the process of, capacity for or outcome of, successful adaption despite challenging circumstances', and by me, here in 2017, as **gumption, guts and a glass-at-least-half-full attitude to life.**

Well, everything you have learned so far will get, or already have got, you off to a good start, and your children may have no trouble with bullying. If, however, they are not so lucky, here are some tried and true ways to help them cope. Most of them apply equally to perpetrator and victim whose problems are so often two sides of the same coin.

These are some of the things that contribute to and develop children's resilience.

Of course enough sleep, exercise and nourishing food, but also: -

1. A close bond with at least one parent or carer.

2. Effective communication - with eyes and ears as well as mouth.

3. Well-understood, consistent rules and consequences.

4. Parents' own example of acceptable behaviour.

5. Adults' positive and can-do attitude.

6. Significant family time together.

7. Good relationships with extended family and/or proxy cousins, uncles and aunts.

8. Opportunities for and appreciation of appropriate responsibilities.

9. Encouragement of hobbies, skills, outside interests and activities.

10. Friendship encouraged with play-dates at home and away.

11. Successful school experience.

12. Social, even service-able community involvement.

Not rocket science and not much you don't know, intend or already do. Well and good, because now you'll see some typical qualities and skills of the resilient child.

• Self-confidence, self-esteem, self-efficacy and self-control.

• Flexibility and adaptability to change.

• Good communication and problem-solving skills.

• Sense of purpose and possibilities.

Ability to make realistic plans, to bear disappointment, learn from mistakes, keep on trying and, perhaps the best gift of all: to make and keep good friends.

This child is well prepared for most of life's hazards, challenges and opportunities. There is, however, more parents can do to help their children avoid or cope with bullying.

To foster this kind of resilience, here's some advice from Tom Thelen, Banardo's, Rowntree's research and my own experience; starting with a few important don'ts.

1. Don't over protect your children: don't remove all obstacles from their path; don't rush to pick them up when they fall; don't make a big fuss over small hurts; don't clean up, pick up, tidy up things (e.g. scribbles, spills, toys) they are capable of doing themselves; don't blame something or someone else for their failures, and don't let tears get them off sanctions and established responsibilities.

2. Do let them learn from their mistakes.

3. Do practice problem-solving in "what-would-you-do-if" kind of discussions (including bullying) that give time and respect for their contribution.

4. Do also encourage them to find solutions to their actual problems before, or instead of, offering your own. Ditto for disputes with siblings or other children.

5. Do ask for and acknowledge the reasons and feelings when anger or distress results in bad behaviour; then encourage them to come up with a better solution, and even an appropriate consequence.

6. Try re-framing adversity as a challenge instead of a disaster.

> I'm thinking of the flooded road home from a long-ago pantomime trip when the car stalled in water almost up to the door. Pitch dark, pouring rain, four small children all tired and hungry; no other traffic, just the light of a farm a couple of fields away. 'Ok, kids, this is what we call a real adventure'. Macs and boots on, splash-splosh, oohs and aahs all the muddy way; tea, cake and warm fire, farmer's tractor to the rescue; then safe home with a good story for all family and friends. Same time next year: unanimous opinion: 'Hope it's going to be another adventure'.

7. Do give your children opportunities for independence, e.g. budgeting their own pocket money, walking unaccompanied to a corner shop or home from the school bus.

8. Do encourage their sense of efficacy from mastering tasks, and confidence in their own ability by supervised exposure to risks, like walking along walls, climbing fences or trees.

9. Do display their art and craft work even if not particularly skilled; publicity is a good motivator to improve. In case of school work, beware of undue praise setting a standard not shared by teachers or peers.

10. Do play all sorts of games: of luck or skill, indoors and out, solo and team; for the experience of competition, cooperation, winning, losing, camaraderie and taking turns.

175

11. Do let them experience varied social roles, such as host, guest, diner-out, audience, organiser or referee.

12. Do consider enrolment in a martial arts class for the self-discipline, control and respect achieved by the famous movie's Karate Kid.

Children often feel ashamed and reluctant to admit being bullied, but if you have reason to suspect yours is; first make sure it's not by an older brother or sister. Bullying between siblings is not common, but may result from festering resentment of unequal attention given to a younger child, which has already been discussed in the section on siblings.

It is much more likely to occur at school which is why all UK state schools are required to have an anti-bullying policy. The best of these address the problems of both perpetrator and victim with frank in-class discussion, role play, trust exercises, team games and 'buddy-pairing up'. So for school bullying it would be well worth contacting the counsellor or principal.

Meanwhile it may help to invite a popular class-mate or (what worked for a friend of mine) even the actual bully for supervised play/games and an especially nice tea.

The last resort for persistent bullying may be home education, a change of school or move to a different neighbourhood. With so much effective prevention, however, I believe you won't need any such - though of course not actual - cure.

MOBILE PHONES

Forty years ago mobile phones were few and far between; designed for only off-base communication, and about the size of an adult shoe.

Before they were issued to social workers making unaccompanied evening visits, I used to imagine, for some dark, mean-street threat, holding an actual shoe to my ear and pretending to dial 999.

Nowadays the tiny, multi-purpose off-spring of those first phones out-number the population of many countries (including UK and USA) and altogether of the whole world.

As they took off in the 1980s, there was much concern about possible brain damage from prolonged or continuous exposure to their emitted radiation. Then second generation mobiles and those that followed were so much improved that, in 2014, the World Health Organisation reported: 'No adverse health effects are established as being caused by mobile phone use.'

Even so, like many historical inventions (industrial machinery, television, cars; even bicycles), the mobile phone can be either a blessing or bane, depending on its responsible use. Encouragement of this and all such milestone privileges is the parent's responsibility.

You don't need me to point out the advantages of their instant communication, information and amusement, or the corresponding risks like loss of privacy, sleep, reading time, family shared time and, not least, mobile phone abuse.

Naturally these disadvantages are going to worry parents, especially those (probably most) who are less tech-savvy than their kids. For them, fortunately, there is plenty of online information and good advice to be found on sites like: commonsensemedia.org connectsafely.org, and Parents' Top 5 Questions About Mobile Phones.

Please keep in mind, though, it's not technical sophistication, but good communication, firmness and fairness that best helps children avoid these temptations and risks: in other words your behaviour management. With its main points and principles already on board, you may still need some guidance about the when, where, how and what-if decisions you will need to make.

Let's start with the when, as in what's the right age for a child's first own mobile phone? While still at home, most parents don't see any need. Once in day-care or primary school, though, two-way communication is obviously useful for missing homework, changed pick-up times, play dates and after-school activities. A simple function phone is sufficient for this kind of thing; easy to operate, useful to learn on and cheap to replace when, almost inevitably, lost.

It won't be long, though, before your child comes across a class-mate's smartphone and begins a pester campaign which, with your own odd-man-out memories, may be hard to resist. Considering the distraction, though, of on-tap puzzles and games; the discovery of facts, fashions and 'friendships' unsuitable for young children, my advice is to stand firm about a phone upgrade at least until secondary school. There, according to a 2012 report from the Royal Statistical Society, 49% of 11-12, and 68% of 13-14 year-olds have their own smartphone. No doubt by now there'd be more, but even then it seems many parents were 'just going with the flow'.

High school attendance, however, is not a guarantee of maturity; young people don't suddenly become mature on that first day of term. It's a gradual process of acquired skills, responsibilities, initiatives and enough independence to enjoy their own company, projects and activities. This process takes more or less time, depending on a child's personality and circumstances, and without a near fit between her/his technical and social skills, you'd be right to expect inappropriate use and hold off a while for the smartphone, explaining your concerns and possible ways they may be addressed.

Meanwhile all relevant professionals recommend thorough preparation for and supervision of this, so far their most expensive, useful and potentially harmful possession.

Most eight year-olds are more tech-savvy than I (clearly the wrong generation to give advice about social media). The likes of Twitter, texting and Facebook all seem to me second best to real face to face communication, and even voice to voice chat on the phone.

The recommended preparation and supervision, however, do make perfect sense to me.

For example: –

1. Frank discussion, understanding and acceptance of all previously mentioned advantages and risks.

2. Approved privacy-settings and permitted number and expense of apps.

3. Recognition of and distinction between acceptable and inappropriate contacts and sites.

4. Consideration of site blocking.

5. The minimum age (13) for the use of Facebook.

6. Permitted times: how much, how long, where and when (e.g. not at school or meal table, not when driving or in the presence of visitors; not before homework, or in bed after lights out, when the phones' batteries, as the children's, need to be recharged.

7. For stranger and other dangers: no personal ID (name, phone number, home or email address to be given without parents' approval).

8. Identifying the risks of sexting.*

9. Recognised consequences for misuse, like further time restriction or periods of actual confiscation.

In time, no doubt, children will find ways to get round some of these rules but, from your 'thorough' preparation, also ways to protect themselves from harm.

* Sexting is defined by the National Society for the Prevention of Cruelty to Children as the sharing of 'sexual, naked or semi-naked images or videos, or sexually explicit messages.'

Around 1 in 7 young people have taken naked or semi-naked pictures of themselves. Over half went on to share them with someone else.

Since 2016, according to ChildLine, it is illegal in England and Wales for anyone under the age of 18 to take, send or receive a sexual photo, even if it is a 'selfie'. This means the police may follow up any incident that comes to their attention; though, if both participants 'are under 18 and in a healthy relationship, it's unlikely [they] would want to take things further'. This is because the law is not there to punish but to protect young people from the sort of risks listed here by the NSPCC.

Loss of privacy: Having no control of images and how they are shared.

Blackmail: An offender may threaten to share the pictures with the child's family and friends unless given money or more images.

Bullying: If images are shared with their peers or in school, the child may be bullied.

Unwanted attention: Images posted online can attract the attention of sex offenders who know how to search for, collect and modify them.

Emotional distress: Children can feel embarrassed and humiliated. If they are very distressed this could lead to self-harm or even suicide.

In many - perhaps most - families, this is the last sort of thing adolescents want to discuss with their parents who may have no idea if or when it has occurred, so please at least introduce the subject in your 'preparation', and recommend Child-line for the chance of a private conversation and advice.

Before sexting the most dreaded and most widely publicised risk from smartphones was, and maybe still is cyber bullying. This may be a technical step-up for the same playground victim and bully, or entry-level for first-timers with similar personality and problems as those involved in the offline bullying already discussed.

Whether or not this is true of anonymous 'trollers', theirs is a bigger stage for the victims' public torment by any amount of copy-cat bullying. Same problem, but worse in terms of exposure, duration, accountability (none), pain and distress. Cyber bullying is not only vicious, but also illegal, and in case it occurs in your family, you can get really helpful information and advice from the online sites listed below on page 209.

Meanwhile it's worth taking another look at the BULLYING section for resilience factors that protect children from this, and many other of life's arrows and slings, as well as the References and Resources section, in order to prepare them for the smart use of their must-have smartphone.

DIVORCE AND SEPARATION

Divorce, which was once a rare and social disgrace now ends almost half of all marriages in the UK. To be more exact, the Office of National Statistics figure for 2016 is 42% after an average of 11.7 years.

There are all sorts of legal, political and social reasons for this increase which will not be explored here as my personal and professional interest is in the effect on children of their parents' divorce.

There are no accurate figures for co-habiting relationships, but most of what follows applies equally to them.

Except in cases of revealed adultery, parents' decision to separate rarely comes out of the blue. It is usually taken as the sad or angry solution to the disappointment or resentment over the unmet needs of couples no longer in love.

School age children will have class mates from broken families and, recognising the signs, may try to make peace between quarrelling parents, distract them with their own problems, bad behaviour or even ask 'Are you going to get a divorce?'. Old enough to ask is old enough for an honest answer: 'Yes', 'No' or 'Maybe, but if we do, it's not your fault (a common misbelief); mummy and daddy love you very much and you'll be able to keep seeing us both, only not in the same house'.

Such a drastic step with life changing consequences for the whole family might be avoided with the help of joint counselling or therapy. Relate, though, an agency well known in the UK for successful marriage guidance also provides counselling for a 'successful' divorce.

However distressing marriage break-up is for parents, they, or at least one, have some choice in the matter, while their helpless children may be equally or even more distressed. This begs the question whether it's better to stay in, or delay leaving, a bad marriage for their sake. In my opinion, if sincere efforts with therapy or counselling have failed, probably not, as expressed and even suppressed resentment or misery do more harm than good to all concerned.

Nowadays in the UK, to avoid court time spent on conflicting or inappropriate demands, divorcing couples must first attend a Mediation Assessment Meeting. This is not to sort out relationship problems, but to ascertain whether they can make acceptable financial and child care arrangements without going to court. Individual or joint follow-up sessions will be offered; not compulsory, but at about a quarter the cost of a court hearing, may be well worth while. In either case it's best to come prepared with plans for your own wants and needs as well as those of your children. Some help with this may be found online at www.lawpack.co.uk/separation-and-divorce (unless there are child protection issues, the separation of co-habiting parents requires no registration or record).

So when to tell the children? Certainly before whichever parent moves out, but not until you have both agreed and made arrangements for their care. Usually their first concern is which one they are going to live with, and the second: how, when and where are they going to spend time with the absent one? Unless the court is involved this is your decision, likely to depend as much on finances, housing and travel, as on any remaining good will.

The most interesting arrangement I've heard of is the 'birds' nest' where the children stay in the family home (keeping the same school, activities and friends), while the parents, with separate accommodation, take turns in looking after them. Of course this is only possible for those with enough money for housing and convenient jobs, but anyone also interested can get more information (including the pros and cons) online at www.custodyzen.com/divorce-terms/birds-nest-custody.

Best of the more usual arrangements is accommodation for the departing parent, roomy enough and close enough for regular, predictable day and over-night visiting. To sustain the relationship with young children this can be brief, but should be frequent, while teenagers are often satisfied with longer intervals between also longer visits.

Of course finances, employment and available housing will influence or even dictate your plans but, if there is any room for choice, it's a case of the nearer the easier and better, the further the harder and worse for the whole family.

Least best of all for children is the situation where either parent chooses or is obliged to move right away. The one with custody (often mother) may want to return to her distant family; the breadwinner (usually father) may have better job prospects far away – even abroad – where phone calls, Facebook and Skype are poor substitutes for the physical contact and warmth of the 'real thing'. However pressing your wants and needs, they should be, and in court would be, carefully weighed with the welfare of the children in mind.

Many separated parents have found a sort of second family in their local Gingerbread friendship group. Gingerbread is a UK charity in aid of all single parents, offering, as needed, professional pre and post-divorce, legal, financial, housing and child care advice, as well as continuing help and support. Friendship groups are formed by single fathers and mothers living in the same area who arrange picnics, parties, games and trips; share experience, ideas and strategies while making (both adults and children) new friends and gaining confidence from being all in the same boat. For more information visit membership@gingerbread.org.uk or phone 0800 0184318.

Anyway, after divorce, final or even trial separations, absent parents' best chance of a good relationship with their kids is to have at least a cooperative one with their spouse. That should include being on the same page for what to tell them about the situation: past, present - and future, as far as it's known. This won't take as long as all the 'when' preparation, but it's equally important to help them cope with such a massive change in their lives. So, 'before whichever parent moves out', separately or together, do explain it as previously suggested, with updates if need be.

There may be circumstances that justify splitting the children up; one or more going with each parent. They should be allowed to discuss this, but not asked to make a choice. That would only add guilt to the now double loss of daily sibling contact and support.

Whatever living and visiting arrangements you make, here are some important things to keep in mind and ways to make the best of what you all do still have.

1. Older children probably have less need than younger ones for a 'Why (are you doing this?)' explanation. For all of them, though, it's best to keep it simple ('too many disagreements/another relationship'), to skip the details (not their business), to avoid spiteful or bitchy remarks, and to accept the shared blame that has nothing to do with them.

> I don't remember what unkind or unhelpful words were exchanged between me and my husband shortly after our separation, nor which of us actually said them, but I'll never forget nine year-old Peter clasping one each of our hands across his chest and pleading 'Can't you at least not be mean to each other?' It was a lasting wake-up call for us both.

2. Beware: visitation is one of the most common and critical trouble spots. Things like late pick up or return, and broken promises will soon put paid to any cooperative or flexible relationship. Needless to say keep to the plan and, in unforeseen circumstances, remember the phone.

3. Another hot spot is child maintenance. Sometimes there are valid reasons for a temporary delay that won't strain a cooperative relationship, but for persistent non-payment you can apply, or reapply, through social services or a solicitor, to the court.

4. Once you or the court have approved your arrangements, one parent's child care is no business of the other, so by all means show a general interest ('How was it?' or 'Did you have a good time?') but don't nit-pick about details. If you have reasons for concern they should be addressed with the other parent, social services, solicitor or court, not with the child.

5. Don't try to compete for your children's loyalty with less discipline and more treats. Of course they will take advantage but, from a very young age, they respect just limits and know the difference between unconditional and cupboard love.

In this situation myself, I was determined not to be a soft touch parent but to stand my ground about manners and good behaviour.

The first summer was spent in a caravan on my brother's farm. There, Peter, himself adjusting to the situation, would often complain about my firmness spoiling his holiday.

One morning, with a busy day ahead, the wafting smell of breakfast toast gave rise to the following conversation: -

P: Plenty of butter, Mum, OK?

Me: High time you were out of bed, and able to butter your own toast, OK?

P: (at table, reaching for the butter with a sheepish grin) I hope you realise this is going to spoil my whole holiday.

Hallelujah for such good humoured self-awareness, and well done him.

6. Be prepared: in the last few hours of even the most successful visit children often prefer their own company to yours. It seems they need some emotional space between their two – especially if still contentious – lives. In that case the best you can do is supply some suitable comics or magazines and just back off.

7. Sooner or later, either or both parents may find a new partner and start another family which your child(ren) will need to get along with, so do avoid bad-mouthing the newcomer and don't ask the kids to act as spies.

8. Where there are step or half siblings it's in everyone's interest for them to get along together and this may be encouraged by visits to each other's home.

I've known some first and second families getting together for BBQs and picnics, with children and parents becoming good friends. For others, probably most, this may be asking too much, so just do your best with numbers 1 – 8.

These are no rules for a situation you didn't sign up for when you got married; just a set of guide lines from which you may want to, or have to, pick and choose. Even with all of them in sight, though, sometimes you'll lose your footing in this unfamiliar territory but, with self-control and your children's best interest at heart, it is still and also possible to be, in Dr. Winnicott's terms, good enough (divorced) parents.

PETS

Most children would like to have a pet, and that's what I would like for them as well. Why? Not only for the pleasure and pride of ownership, but also for the many life lessons involved in their care: the daily responsibility for feeding and hygiene; in some cases exercise and in others the child's first experience of mating, birth and death which may help later understanding and acceptance of such things in their human family.

A good age for children's first pet? What counts here is not so much age as maturity, which you can judge from their interest and understanding in discussion of a possible pet's particular needs. Where there is already a family pet this may be apparent, or anyway tested, by their concern for and cooperation with its care.

The fact of friends and classmates having this or that pet is not proof of your own child's readiness which is something only you can judge.

What kind of pet to start with?

Obviously things like in and out-door space, parents' employment and child's day care will influence, and perhaps limit the choices, but even a small flat will have room for a gold fish or stick insect, neither needing much attention, but still enough to prepare for whatever mammal may come next.

My own preference is for pets that appreciate human contact more than wild freedom, which would rule out most fish, rodents and birds, except that many of these are bred in, and for, a life of captivity.

When I was six or seven years old my older sister was given a pretty yellow canary that I felt sorry for, always stuck in a cage. One day I found a ball of red wool, tied the end to one of its legs and let it fly out and away from the window. After a while (I don't remember how long), winding the wool back onto the ball, I do remember the horror of finding on the end of it, just one tiny leg. Fortunately for me, my good intention was recognised and I was not punished. Fortunately for the canary, and proving the point about captivity, it returned by itself and lived several more years happily hopping about the cage on its remaining leg.

For any pet there are expenses to be considered: not just the purchase price, and the extra mouth to feed, but also vets bills and in some cases kennel fees when you are away on holiday.

Anyway it's a good idea to prepare young children with story books about their chosen creature, and for older ones, perhaps an instruction leaflet or magazine. Even so and of course, you'll need to supervise and sometimes take part in their pet care.

I have little experience of fish, rodents or birds, and none at all of reptiles, but I know of many children more than happy with mice, gerbils, hamsters, guinea-pigs and rabbits which have their parents' space/time problems nicely solved. For these you can get useful online information and advice at:

www.healthline.com/8BestPetsforKids
www.parents.com/PetsforKids

I'm on safer ground with cats which, over the years, have given much pleasure and comfort to my own and other people's children.

Occasionally little Peter was sent in tears to his room where our old black cat would snuggle up on the bed and gently pat his face; 'Black Mummy' according to him, 'much nicer' than me. Beware though, the boot may be on the other foot when previously childless parents bring home a new baby, their darling cat may visit it's cradle or cot with bad ('I'm your better baby') intent or just ('Let's get acquainted') curiosity, that could cause some fear or harm.

Kittens, of course, are especially adorable, and a good, safe place to get them (grown cats as well unless you want them to breed) is any of the rescue charities listed in the phone book or online. They are all health checked, inoculated and, if the right age, neutered; if not (as this is required), they will be referred to your local vet with a 10% discount for that and any further treatment fees: typical 2017 cost (that includes the neutering) is about £60.

Dogs: all the qualities that gained their reputation as man's best friend, make them also good pets for children.

Remember being introduced to 'perfect Penny': such a good mother to her pups, but also a well-loved family pet.

Of course they need more attention, training and exercise than cats, but this is well repaid by their responsiveness, fun and games, loyalty and often do-or-die protection of their owner's life, limb and home.

Years ago, on family walks, our Scotty-cross mongrel would circle on his little legs round and round us all, keeping stray children off the road, and any other approaching dog safely out of reach. A sound sleeper though, he didn't move a muscle the night our car was stolen from the driveway, but did do his best the next morning to scare off the investigating police. Maybe not the smartest dog in the world, but certainly one with his heart in the right place.

Although the aggressiveness of some breeds (like Rottweilers and pit bulls) is often blamed on bad training rather than bad character, it's probably better to play safe with well-known child-friendly breeds such as Labradors, retrievers, cocker spaniels and pugs. These, whole or part bred, may be bought from rescue kennels but, considering 'bad training', their past history should first be checked.

Pedigree breeds are always more and, often very, expensive. Buyers should, though, beware of low-cost puppy farms: many have too few staff for individual handling and 'socialising', and some have even been found importing foreign puppies with fake registration and health certificates, resulting (one case I know) in over £3,000 of vet bills.

If you are not able or ready yet to take full responsibility of a dog for your child, s/he might like the chance to walk, groom and dog-sit other peoples', or help at a rescue kennel, some of which also want foster-carers for waiting-to-be re-homed pups. Not only a useful experience but, keeping in mind that 'a dog is not just for Christmas', any such involvement would be a good test of your child's interest and commitment to the 'real thing'.

Now for ponies and horses: for some reason, after puberty more girls than boys take to recreational (as opposed to competitive) riding, though both gain, from either kind, considerable physical (health), social (friendship) and personal (confidence and self-respect) benefits and skills.

For those with just imagination sparked by books and films, or envy of equestrian friends, it's a good idea to start – and test their interest – with riding lessons from a reputable stable where grooming, tack care and mucking-out are part of the learning experience, and staff are likely to have, or know of, suitable ponies and horses for sale.

When it comes to ownership, though, the one-off price of purchase is the least of the costs involved. Stabling, summer pasture, winter feed, harness, regular shoeing and vet bills all need to be taken into account. No wonder riding is often considered a pastime of the very rich.

Even so, many far from rich young riders work after school, in the holidays and later take second jobs to buy and keep their own horse: intelligent and loyal as any dog, and just as good a life-long companion and friend.

By now you can tell which animals I know best and find the most rewarding, but my final and concluding reason for wanting children to have any kind of pet is that I've known many who regret that they didn't, but none not very glad that they did.

GAMES

Fun and games? Maybe, can be, sometimes, never. I know some parents who groan at the very word, and others so competitive that they just have to win. In both cases they are missing out on a lot of family fun; also missing the point already made about the mental, physical and social value to children of playing games.

Of course not all games are right for all children but, depending on their age, talents and interests, there are plenty any of them can play with pleasure and fun. From quite an early age they will get that most games are competitive, and naturally want to win. So it's a good idea to start with those calling for more luck than skill (like snakes and ladders, happy families, bronco and fish) that give everyone an equal chance.

For indoor games like Monopoly, Rumikub, Boggle, and out-door treasure and scavenger hunts, hare and hounds, it often helps a young or unconfident child to pair up with an older sibling or friend. Then there's Pelmanism (matching turned-up picture cards) with mini wins for each ongoing success; also hide & seek when they actually want to be found. For the next level, pick-up sticks, dominoes, noughts and crosses and snap are all mixed luck and skill games that you could occasionally or often, discreetly lose.

When I was still working with children, a timid 8 year old only child always chose to end his play sessions with peg-board noughts and crosses which I mostly let him win. At first he seemed happy with this, but after some genuine successes on other activities, he began pointing out better moves for me, and taking charge of the score. Of course I was more than happy with that.

Sooner or later, though, and certainly by school age, children should be able to take losing in their stride. That itself is a big success, likely due to the pleasure given and the confidence gained by early wins; while too many losses could put them off games altogether.

By then most children will have spent hours playing games on their i-Pad or phone. Peace and quiet for them and their parents but, for social skills, the virtual world is no match for the real thing.

So what's to be done about a loser's disappointment, anger or sulks? Once again, prevention is better than cure, and following the previous suggestions you'll already have made a good start.

1. With a game in progress, cheer any small gains, sympathise with set-backs, praise - even reward - all efforts, patience and perseverance.

2. No use reminding them it's only a game; instead remind yourself from the class about **play being children's work** which of course they're going to take seriously.

3. So a serious reaction to your own losses ('oh well, better luck next time') and even a humorous one (mock pouts and moans) would be good examples for your child.

4. If a child is too young or too upset for reason or humour, trouble may still be avoided by sympathy and a switch to another, easier game.

5. Cure: the first rule is keep your cool: one upset or angry person is quite enough and a like-for-like response is good for neither parent nor child.

6. Game over, sulking can be ignored while you get on with something else, and tempers can be dealt with by a period of time out to cool down.

7. In both cases, explain your intention to wait till they are ready to make a fresh start.

All these measures will help prepare your children for the rough and tumble of school yard play, for class-room competition and the teamwork of organised sport.

Team sport involves another level of challenge and skill, with more to learn, more to teach and more at stake in terms of popularity, reputation and pride. Most sports have cub clubs for young children, and while in Canada, I took five year-old Peter to see ice-hockey cubs in action.

Right from the start parents in the stands were shouting hateful instructions the worst of which (though not by much) was, 'Come on Andy, break his f@$#!^% leg!' Needless to say that's a club we did not join. Fortunately there were plenty of others, more sociable and well managed; focussing less on winning or losing, than just, and fairly, playing the game.

8. Not all games are, or need be, competitive: for solitaire (marbles) and patience (cards) the only challenge for the player is to beat his/her previous best score.

9. Finding and piecing together cut-out picture post cards from a jumbled heap can be an individual or cooperative game: for 2-3 year olds cards cut in half, for 4-6 year- olds in four, and over 6's in six uneven shapes.

10. Remember those paper cups that can be built into low, high, wide and wonderful walls, towers and castles by individuals, pairs or groups of children of any age.

11. There is plenty of fun and no winners or losers in games like heads, bodies, legs and good old 'consequences'.

Less well known, but a good game for any age including adults, PREDICAMENTS is worth explaining here.

Any number of players in a circle are given two pieces of paper, one with the letter Q, the other an A in the top corner.

Under Q they write a question beginning with 'What would you do if...?' (e.g., If you missed the school bus home? Or if a boy tries to kiss you?)

Under A they write an answer beginning with 'I would...' (e.g., I would call mum to come and get me or I would tell him to get lost)

Next, all the Qs are passed to the person on the right; all As to the one on the left, so everyone has mismatched questions and answers which, read aloud, are always amusing, and often surprisingly apt.

(Children, too young to write, can join in by whisper-dictating their contributions the adult in charge.)

---

12. For car journeys, wet days and waiting rooms, here are some other pen-and-paper games with challenges of observation, numbers, language and hand-eye coordination that can usefully and pleasantly pass the time.

CAR JOURNEY LOOK-OUT

HOUSE WITH TWO CHIMNEYS

BLACK DOG

CARAVAN

MOTOR BIKE

BLACK AND WHITE COW

CHICKENS OR DUCKS

CHILD

GREEN CAR

LORRY

WHITE HORSE

RED LETTER BOX

TRAFFIC LIGHTS

FLAG

BUS

BICYCLE

WOODEN GATE

SEAGULL

CHURCH

PLANE OR HELICOPTER

BRIDGE

DONKEY

CAT

Of course you could make up your own list of typical or likely local features.

QUIZ: FOR EACH DESCRIPTION GIVE TWO WORDS THAT MUST RHYME
PTO FOR ANSWERS

1.   MOGGY AFTER A VERY BIG MEAL

2.   TWO-TIMES FIVE ADULT MALES

3.   UNHAPPY FATHER

4.   COSY CARPET

5.   OVERGROWN PORKER

6.   EXTRA SEAT

7.   DO's AND DON'Ts IN THE CLASS ROOM

8.   ABSOLUTELY CORRECT

9.   YOUR PEEP HOLE

10. COLLECTION OF RECIPES

11. EQUAL PORTION

12. MORE CHEERFUL WIREY LITTLE DOG

13. NOT THIS MALE SIBLING

14. FEBRUARY'S FOOLISH ARCHER

15. AMUSING COINS

16. BLOND LOCKS

17. ANGRY MANAGER

18. ONLY MALE CHILD

19. CHEERFUL BLOKE

20. LIGHT IN A TENT

QUIZ ANSWERS

1. FAT CAT
2. TEN MEN
3. SAD DAD
4. SNUG RUG
5. BIG PIG
6. SPARE CHAIR
7. SCHOOL RULES
8. QUITE RIGHT
9. MY EYE
10. COOK BOOK
11. FAIR SHARE
12. MERRIER TERRIER
13. OTHER BROTHER
14. STUPID CUPID
15. FUNNY MONEY
16. FAIR HAIR
17. CROSS BOSS
18. ONE SON
19. HAPPY CHAPPIE
20. CAMP LAMP

Perhaps you could make up some more for your friends.

THE STORY OF TIBS, with sound effects by the children.

Once upon a time there was a very naughty little cat called Tibs. He lived on a farm where his idea of fun was chasing the **hens** around the yard, sneaking up to bite the tail of the **pig,** pulling bits of wool off the **sheep**, hiding in the hay manger to frighten the **horse** and at milking time, hanging on the tail of every **cow**. And when he should have been catching **mice**, he would take a ride on the farmer's **tractor** instead.

One day, while bothering the **hens**, he was given a taste of his own medicine by the **cockerel** who chased him out of the yard and into a field where the only place he could escape was up a very tall tree and stay there safely out of reach.

At supper time, when the farmer's wife called for him, he was nowhere to be seen, but after a few minutes she did hear his **cry** and found him perched up on the topmost branch. Too high for the farm ladder, and no way was he going to come down as long as the **cockerel** was standing guard.. The farmers wife was afraid to leave him to come down later in case he got eaten by a **fox**. So she phoned the fire brigade who rushed out in their big red truck with it's **blaring horn** which frightened little **cat** even more than the **cockerel**.

What do you think the nice fireman said when he'd brought Tibs down? - - - - Yes, and 'that should teach you a lesson, you naughty little **cat**.' And so it did. From that day on, Tibs never bothered the **hens**,the **pig**, the **sheep**, the **horse** or the **cows** ever again. Instead he just spent his time outside catching **mice**, and indoors, by the fire, **purring** to his heart's content.

Dot to Dot Game

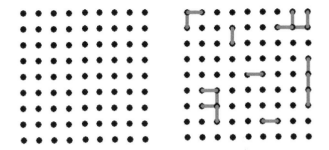

1. The object of the game is to claim and name the most boxes on the grid.

2. Two to four players take turns joining, with a single vertical or horizontal line, two adjacent dots.

3. The player who adds a fourth side claims that box and takes another turn.

4. All players need to beware of adding a third side anywhere.

5. As the grid begins to fill, any added fourth side may become the third side of an adjoining box, allowing the player to have another turn, then possibly more.

6. The game ends when no more lines can be drawn.

7. For younger children you may want to start with a smaller grid.

Paradoxically, games <u>and</u> the fun which keeps children on board, are worth taking seriously because the child of a family that plays together is learning more, and more important, things than just the rules of any or many a game.

AFTERWORD

That's it, then. What a long way we've come, together: from the first understanding of children's wants and needs; through all sorts of ups and downs, finding how to help them become responsible, capable, sociable adults; at ease with themselves, their families and able to take in stride the challenges and opportunities of the great game of life.

REFERENCES AND RESOURCES

Though help-lines and phone numbers are apt to change, you should be able to find relevant information and advice by just entering some key words of any particular concern. Meanwhile, all that follows is valid at the time of publication.

REFERENCES

Page 10: The Oxford English Dictionary.

Page 12: Dr. Thomas A Harris: author of I'm OK, You're OK.

Page 28: Roger Graef: 19197, producer of documentary film: "Breaking the Cycle."

Page 53: Dr. Benjamin Spock: 1940s author of Baby and Child Care, and other parenting books.

Page 56: Albert Einstein: his views on reading to children.

Page 58: Lotte Bailyn: Fellow of the American Psychological Association.

Page 69: James Baldwin: American novelist, essayist, playwright, poet, and social critic.

Page 72: Jesuits: Famous for their claim: 'Give me a child till he is seven, and I'll give you the man.'

Page 80: Dr. Donald Winnicott: Twice President of the British Psychoanalytical Society.

Page 88: Rosemary Van Norman: Author of <u>Help for Thumb-Sucking Children</u>.

Page 91: Alison Scott-Wright: Author of <u>The Sensational Baby Sleep Plan</u>.

Page 93: Dr Mario Motta: (AMA Council of Science and Public Health) Research on sleep.

Page 106: Ray Lacy: Clinical Psychologist.

Page 138: Katherine Whitehorn: Author of <u>Cooking in A Bed-sitter</u>.

Page 171: Tom Thelen: Founder of Victim-proof Bullying Prevention Programs (USA).

Page 172: Masters *et al*: For the Joseph Rowntree Trust, his paper on childhood resilience.

Page 178: The Royal Statistical Society: figures for the ownership (by age) of mobile phones.

Page 184: Mediation Assessment Meeting: Now mandatory for divorcing couples.

ADHD
• The Attention Deficit Disorder Information and Support Service (ADDISS) telephone: 020 8952 2800.

AUTHOR
• www.virginiahobart.co.uk

• www.childrenbehave.co.uk

BED TIME
• For immediate advice: alisonscott-wright.com/my-Services

• www.sleepcouncil.co.uk

• www.telegraph.co.uk/two thirds of children not getting enough sleep (23rd April 2012).

BED WETTING
• www.nhs.uk/Conditions/Bedwetting

• ERIC (Education and Resources for Improving Childhood Incontinence) www.eric.org.uk

BITING
• families.naeyc.org/understanding-and-responding-children-who-bite

BULLYING
• http://www.anti-bullyingalliance.org.uk/advice/parents-carers.aspx

• Deletecyberbullying.org

DIVORCE AND SEPARATION
• www.lawpack.co.uk/separation-and-divorce

• www.custodyzen.com/divorce-terms/birds-nest-custody

• www.relate.org.uk

• membership@gingerbread.org.uk

• Help-line telephone: 0808 8020925

DUMMY OR THUMB
• Thumbsie.co.uk

• www.thumbusters.com

MASTURBATION
• www.nhs.uk/chq/Pages/1684.aspx

MOBILE PHONES
• www.connectsafely.org

• www.commonsensemedia.org

• https://www.parentmap.com/.../dos-and-donts-for-parents-of-first-time-cell-phone-use

• deletecyberbullying.org

• puresight.com (cyberbullying/dos-and-don't-for-cyber-bullying-victims)

• www.nspcc.org.uk/sexting

• email help@nspcc.org.uk (phone 0808 800 5000)

• ChildLine: www.childline.org.uk (phone 0800 1111)

• CEOP: Child Exploitation & Online Protection Centre - internet safety www.ceop.police.uk

OUTDOOR ACTIVITIES
• www.amazon.co.uk/What-Look-Ladybird-Nature/dp/0721400965

• https://en.wikipedia.org/wiki/Oberver's_Books

PETS
• www.healthline.com/8BestPetsforKids

• www.parents.com/PetsforKids

PICKY EATERS
• www.bda.uk/foodfacts

READING TO CHILDREN
• www.raisesmartkid.com/benefitsofreadingtoyourchild

SEX EDUCATION
• 'Facts of Life': www.fpa.org.uk

• The Sex Education Forum: www.ncb.org.uk/sef

• NHS campaign: 'Sex Worth Talking About'

• The Speakeasy Sex Education Course at Cornwall's Healthy Schools. Telephone: 01209 313 419

SIBLINGS
• greatergood.berkeley.edu/raising.../siblings

• www.attachfromscratch.com/siblings-without-rivalry imaginaryfriend/sibling:newsmedical.net/news/200906 03/imaginaryfriends

SPECIAL NEEDS
- www.actionforkids.org

- www.childrenwithdisabilities.inf/parenting

- www.citizensadvice.org.uk/young-people/childreninneed

- info@downs-syndrome.org.uk
  (Telephone: 0333 1212300)

- www.epilepsysociety.org.uk/parents

- www.mencap.org.ukchildren-with learning-disabilities

- www.autism.org.uk/services/local.aspx

- www.scope.org.uk/support/families

- Support for any kind of disability, including home-adaptation grants, telephone: 0808 800 3333

- www.tommys.org/pregnancy-information/premature-Birth

TANTRUMS
- www.familylives.org.uk/advice/understanding-and-dealing-with-tantrums (Helpline telephone: 0808 8002222)

- Therapeutic Bop Bag: www.superdairyboy.com/3-D_Bob_Bags

- www.nhsinform/tantrums.

BED TIME
• The Sensational Baby Sleep Plan by Alison Scott-Wright: Bantam Press (8th Jan, 2010).

BITING
• No Biting by Karen Katz: Grosset & Dunlap Inc., U.S. (3rd March, 2011).

• Teeth are not for Biting by Elizabeth Verdick: Free Spirit Publishing Inc. (1st June, 2003).

DUMMY OR THUMB
• Charlie's Thumb by Rura Mowla-Copley: R Mowla Copley (August 2013).

MASTURBATION
• Textbook of Basic Nursing by Caroline Rosdahl and Mary Kowalski: LWW (28th December, 2011).

OUTDOOR ACTIVITIES
• Happy Holidays by Alix Woods: Truran (17th November, 2006).

PICKY EATERS
• Stressful Feeding by Lucy Cook & Laura Webber: Robinson (20th August, 2015).

• The Good Parenting Food Guide by Jane Ogden: Wiley-Blackwell (25th April, 2014).

READING TO CHILDREN
• The Read Aloud Handbook by James Trelease: Penguin Books (25th July 2006).

SEX EDUCATION

• <u>4+ Mummy Laid an Egg</u> by Babette Cole: Red Fox Books (1st June, 1995).

• <u>4+ Where Willy Went</u> by Nicholas Allan: Red Fox Books (2nd Feb, 2006).

• <u>7+Where Did I Come From?</u> by Peter Mayle & Arthur Robins: Citadel (1st Sept, 1991).

• <u>The Facts of Life Growing Up</u> by Susan Meredith & Robyn Gee: Usborne (26th Sept, 1997).

WHEN TO START BEHAVIOUR MANAGEMENT

• <u>The House of Tiny Tearaways</u> by Dr. Tanya Byron: BBC Active (23rd Nov. 2005).

TELEVISION

WHEN TO START BEHAVIOUR MANAGEMENT

Any one of the following television programmes says it all:

• Nanny 911

• Supernanny

• Three Day Nanny

• House of the Tiny Tearaways

Under each title, programmes can be replayed and episodes seen on YouTube and House of the Tiny Tearaways is also available on video at www.amazon.co.uk/PrimeVideo

213

• Breaking the Cycle: Roger Graef's 1997 film is still relevant today, but £195 a lot to pay for the video which may be available at some libraries.

• The Secret Lives of 4, 5 and 6 year olds: not an actual text reference, but this fly-on-the-wall observation of children at play is a valuable and delightful resource which is occasionally repeated on TV, and can be found online at The Secret Live of 4, 5 and 6 year olds – All 4.

ABOUT THE AUTHOR

At university Virginia Hobart studied sociology, psychology and education which qualified her for social work in English and Canadian schools, hospital wards and local authority departments during the next forty five years.

It was, however, her experience as a mother, foster-mother and family support worker that she learned more about bringing up children than from all her teachers and books.

Towards the end of her career, while working for Devon County Council (Children and Families Department), she contributed to the preparation of prospective adoption and foster parents with a much appreciated evening class on Behaviour Management.

Quite a challenge, in just two and a half hours, to cover such a complex and important subject in a way that would be useful to groups of hopeful couples from all walks of life.

Her solution was to address the principle and purposes of behaviour with easily recognisable examples, and to engage each class in discussion about their own childhood experience, as well as some simple exercises to make particular points. Finally, over coffee, the evening ended with a long list of practical suggestions for the management – or even prevention – of their children's unacceptable behaviour.

After retirement, it occurred to her that the same material could just as well be conveyed in the written, as the spoken, word. And now it is all to be found in this self-help book for the use of prospective and actual parents, whether on their own, in in groups of interested neighbours and friends.

For more information regarding this work or the author, please visit:

www.virginiahobart.co.uk
or
www.childrenbehave.co.uk

Made in the USA
Columbia, SC
06 August 2017